Watch and Wait
A Guide for Advent and Christmas

Jim Branch

So roll up your sleeves, put your mind in gear, be totally ready to receive the gift that's coming when Christ arrives.

~1 Peter 1:13 (The Message)

Preface

Well, here we stand at the beginning of yet another Advent season. Once again we will read the scriptures that encourage us to watch and wait, to pay attention for the coming of the Christ into our lives and our world. Once again we will be called upon to keep our eyes peeled because we never quite know when or where or how God might choose to show up among us or within us.

It is a season that comes along each year, which might cause us take the attitude of "Been there, done that." I mean, what could possibly be different in this year than in all the others? But, although it is true that the season itself never changes, we would be remiss in thinking that there is nothing new for us to look out for this go round. For though the season of Advent never changes, we do.

That is what makes this season — and every Advent season — new and different from the ones of days gone by. It is not because they have changed, it is because we have. We are different people now than we were a year ago. We are in a different place this year than we were the last — be it a little or be it a lot. We have changed, even if those changes are hardly recognizable. We have lived. We have grown. We have been broken. We have been delighted. We have different circumstances and dynamics affecting us. We have different issues pressing on our hearts and souls. We have lost, and in some cases gained, loved ones. Quite simply, we are different people.

And, since we are different people, we should expect that different words and images might speak to us in this new place in which we find ourselves — different from the ones that have spoken to us in the days of Advents past. It seems good and proper to at least acknowledge that at the beginning of our journey together and to consider how it might be true.

How are you different this year than you were the last? What has changed within you? What has changed around you? And what seems to be the same? How do you feel about that? How do you long for Jesus *to come* into your life and your world this year? How do you need him to come? Because the season of Advent always assures us that *he will come*, it is just who he is. So come, Lord Jesus, come!

Introduction

For most of my Christian life I was unaware of the
beautiful way the story of faith retells itself each year
through the church calendar. I knew absolutely nothing
about how each and every year, through its feasts and
celebrations and remembrances, the incredible story of
God's extravagant love for his people is lived out again
and anew by the community of faith. It is an invitation to
us all to journey with Christ — and the people of God — into
a more intimate and vibrant relationship with the One who
made us for himself. It is an invitation for each of us to
enter in to the story once again; to live each season in a way
that gives us a deeper love for, and a stronger faith in, the
God who dreamt us into being.

The beginning of this yearly pilgrimage is the season of
Advent, the season where we watch and wait for the
coming of the Christ. In fact, the word advent comes from
the Latin word *adventus*, which means *coming*. Thus,
during the season of Advent, we are invited to watch and
wait for God's arrival within us and among us, which
makes it a time of intense yearning and deep longing. It is
a time filled with hope and anticipation, a time that reflects
the four hundred years between the Old and New
Testaments when God's people waited for Him to appear,
to speak once again after all the years of silence.

Can you imagine? Four hundred years of silence. Four
hundred years of watching and waiting. How easy it
would have been to have lost hope. How easy it would
have been to be filled with doubt and despair. How easy it
would have been to give up, to lose heart, to stop believing

that God was ever going to show up again. How easy it would have been for us to say, "My master is taking a long time in coming" and begin living by our own rule and our own agenda once again. Advent is the time when we heed the words of Jesus, *"Therefore, keep watch because you do not know on what day your Lord will come."* So during the days and weeks ahead, may we wait with careful attention for his coming, lest when he finally arrives, we miss him altogether.

My prayer for this book is that it would do just that. That it would offer you a traveling companion for this first leg of the journey, as we watch and wait and prepare to receive *the God who comes* — Emmanuel! May he come to you in a real and transforming way in the forty-plus days ahead.

Grace and Peace,

Jim

First Sunday in Advent

Opening Prayer: *Come, Lord Jesus!* Those are the words that you end the scriptures with, O God, and therefore they are the words with which we begin this Advent season. For we long for your coming, Lord Jesus. We long for your coming into our lives and into our families, into our communities and into our world—but mostly we long for your coming into our hearts and souls. Come, Lord Jesus!

Scripture Reading: Isaiah 64:1-9

Oh that you would rend the heavens and come down,
that the mountains might quake at your presence –
as when fire kindles brushwood
and the fire causes water to boil –
to make your name known to your adversaries,
and that the nations might tremble at your presence!
When you did awesome things that we did not look for,
you came down, the mountains quaked at your presence.
From of old no one has heard
or perceived by the ear,
no eye has seen a God besides you,
who acts for those who wait for him.
You meet him who joyfully works righteousness,
those who remember you in your ways.
Behold, you were angry, and we sinned;
in our sins we have been a long time, and shall we be saved?
We have all become like one who is unclean,
and all our righteous deeds are like a polluted garment.
We all fade like a leaf,

and our iniquities, like the wind, take us away.
There is no one who calls upon your name,
*   who rouses himself to take hold of you;*
for you have hidden your face from us,
*   and have made us melt in the hand of our iniquities.*
But now, O Lord, you are our Father;
*   we are the clay, and you are our potter;*
*   we are all the work of your hand.*
Be not so terribly angry, O Lord,
*   and remember not iniquity forever.*
*   Behold, please look, we are all your people. (ESV)*

Journal: What does the image of God *rending the heavens and coming down* stir up within you today?

What excites you about that image?

What terrifies you about it? Why?

Where are you most deeply longing for God to *come down* into your heart and life these days?

Reading for Reflection:
Venite! O Come! It is the cry of the Advent season, as well as the deepest cry of our hearts. And though we may not always be completely aware of its presence, it is still definitely there. It is the part of us that yearns for more. It is the part of us that longs for life and love, for peace and wholeness. We all have a burning desire for God to show up and make his dwelling among us. *O Come* puts the ball squarely in God's court; all we can do is wait.

But the waiting we are called to do during the season ahead is not a passive, lackadaisical type of waiting. It is actually quite the opposite—it is an active, expectant waiting. For as we wait for God to *come*, which we cannot control, we must do some *coming* of our own. We must show up. We must pay attention. We must be fully present, lest we miss him when he finally appears. During this season, even as our hearts sing *O Come, O Come Emmanuel*, our mouths must remind us that our part is to *Come All Ye Faithful.* For unless we *come*, we will never be able to recognize his *coming.*

Closing Prayer: Help me to be attentive, Lord Jesus, to all of the ways and all of the places and all of the people through whom you will come to me today. You are, and have always been, *the God who comes.* Thank you that your heart will not allow you to stay away. Come, Lord Jesus!

Monday
First Week in Advent

Opening Prayer: Lord God, our Heavenly Father, during this season of Advent help us to prepare our hearts for your coming. Come, Lord Jesus! Come and visit your people. We eagerly await your coming. Come, Lord Jesus! Amen.

Scripture Reading: Matthew 25:1-13

At that time the kingdom of heaven will be like ten virgins who took their lamps and went out to meet the bridegroom. Five of them were foolish and five were wise. The foolish ones took their lamps but did not take any oil with them. The wise ones, however, took oil in jars along with their lamps. The bridegroom was a long time in coming, and they all became drowsy and fell asleep.

"At midnight the cry rang out: 'Here's the bridegroom! Come out to meet him!'

"Then all the virgins woke up and trimmed their lamps. The foolish ones said to the wise, 'Give us some of your oil; our lamps are going out.'

"'No,' they replied, 'there may not be enough for both us and you. Instead, go to those who sell oil and buy some for yourselves.'

"But while they were on their way to buy the oil, the bridegroom arrived. The virgins who were ready went in with him to the wedding banquet. And the door was shut.

"Later the others also came. 'Lord, Lord,' they said, 'open the door for us!'

"But he replied, 'Truly I tell you, I don't know you.'"

"Therefore keep watch, because you do not know the day or the hour." (NIV)

Journal: What does the image of the virgins watching for the bridegroom's arrival do within you?

What is significant to you about the oil?

What does that represent in your life?

How is God asking you to *watch* for him during this season?

What does that involve?

Reading for Reflection:

As I read these words from the gospel of Matthew, I can't help but hear God's voice asking me: *"How is your oil level holding out these days? What is it within you that offers fuel to the flame of My Spirit? Is there a yearning inside that causes you to burn with holy longing (zeal) for a deep and rich life with me? It is a life that comes up from your very depths and shines through your eyes and your face and your very being, like a beacon in this dark and desperate world. It is like Moses when he came down from the mountaintop, aglow with the reflection of my glory and delight. What is it that burns within you these days? Does it burn in such a beautiful way that those in this world are automatically drawn to its light, as a moth to a flame? And how are you nurturing this life of the Spirit within you? How are you keeping that oil level full? Do you have enough of it in your heart and soul to shine on indefinitely? Are you overflowing with My Spirit and My presence and My Love? How will you keep watch? How will you pay attention? How will you make sure that you have enough oil? Are you nurturing and caring for this life of My Spirit within you? Take extra special care, my beloved child, to do just that, for then you will live every second of your life in readiness – readiness for my coming."*

Closing Prayer: O Lord, my God, I am so full of care. Not the good and beautiful kind of care, but the kind of care that heightens my insecurities. The kind of care that makes me perform. The kind of care that makes me jockey for position in the lives of the significant and the beautiful. O God, purge this kind of care from my heart and soul! Help me to be full of the kind of care you delight in; care about your kingdom and your glory. Help me to be filled with a desire to seek your approval alone. Help me to live in the truth that I am your Beloved. Let that be the *oil* that fills my heart and causes me to burn with holy zeal for you. Amen.

Tuesday
First Week in Advent

Opening Prayer: Lord, help me to be watchful for your presence in my life and your movement in my world. Help me to not get distracted by the obligations, demands, and activities of this day, but help me to be attentive and alert to you and your greater purposes for my life. Amen.

Scripture Reading: Psalm 130:1-8

Out of the depths I cry to you, Lord;
*   Lord, hear my voice.*
Let your ears be attentive
*   to my cry for mercy.*
If you, O Lord, kept a record of sins,
*   O Lord, who could stand?*
But with you there is forgiveness,
*   therefore you are feared.*
I wait for the Lord, my soul waits,
*   and in his word I put my hope.*
My soul waits for the Lord
*   more than watchmen wait for the morning,*
*   more than watchmen wait for the morning.*
O Israel, put your hope in the Lord,
*   for with the Lord is unfailing love*
*   and with him is full redemption.*
He himself will redeem Israel
*   from all their sins. (NIV, 1982)*

Journal: How does the image of a *watchman waiting for the morning* speak to your life right now?

What does it do within you?

What is it about this image that God wants you to see?

What is unique about *how* a watchman waits for the morning that specifically speaks to you today?

Where in your life does God seem to be asking you to wait for him?

Reading for Reflection:

I don't know about you, but I hate waiting. And I guess the biggest reason why I hate it is because I've never been very good at it. I've always been one of those "let's get this show on the road" type of people. Waiting demands both an attitude and a posture that are the opposite of my normal default mode. In fact, waiting almost completely takes the ball out of my hands. It asks me to let go of my agenda and my control, and to surrender them both to God. And that is a really difficult thing to do.

But maybe the biggest reason that I hate waiting is because, deep down, I am really afraid that whatever, or whoever, I am waiting on will never appear. I mean, what if I just wait forever and nothing ever happens, or no one ever comes? It is a frightening thought.

That is where this Psalm speaks so deeply to my heart and soul. Because the type of waiting that Psalm 130 is talking about—and the type of waiting that the season of Advent calls us to—is the type of waiting where we can rest assured that there will be an arrival. It is not a question of *if*, but a question of *when* and *where* and *how*. That's why we have to pay very careful attention. That's why we have to be like watchmen.

The image of a watchman waiting for the morning is so helpful during this time and this season. A watchman waits for the morning because he knows beyond a shadow of a doubt that the morning will indeed come. All he has to do is wait. That's why I said that waiting *almost* takes the ball completely out of my hands. Because we still determine *how* we will wait. For once the watchman has dealt with the fact that he cannot hasten the morning's arrival, nor can he delay it (thank goodness), only then can he settle down in trust and begin to truly wait for its coming, being both attentive and expectant. So these beautiful words from this Psalm, and the amazing image it contains, are so helpful because they do not just tell us *that* we must wait, but they tell us *how* we must wait. Thanks be to God.

Closing Prayer: May your unfailing love rest upon us, O Lord, even as we watch and wait and put our hope in you. (Psalm 33:22)

Wednesday
First Week in Advent

Opening Prayer: O Lord, my God, help me to live my life *in* you. Awaken me minute-by-minute, day-by-day, to your presence within me and around me. Awaken me to your love and to your care, to your voice and to your Spirit. Help me to come *all awake within*, and when I finally do, help me to find myself in your loving arms. Amen.

Scripture Reading: Romans 13:11-13

But make sure that you don't get so absorbed and exhausted in taking care of all your day-by-day obligations that you lose track of the time and doze off, oblivious to God. The night is about over, dawn is about to break. Be up and awake to what God is doing! God is putting the finishing touches on the salvation work he began when we first believed. We can't afford to waste a minute, must not squander these precious daylight hours in frivolity and indulgence, in sleeping around and dissipation, in bickering and grabbing everything in sight. Get out of bed and get dressed! Don't loiter and linger, waiting until the very last minute. Dress yourselves in Christ, and be up and about! (The Message)

Journal: What things tend to absorb and exhaust you?

What things make you lose track of God each day?

How is the word *asleep* descriptive of your life or spirit these days?

What would it look like to stay spiritually awake during this season?

What reaction do the words *"Dress yourself in Christ, and be up and about"* cause within you?

What does that image look like for you these days?

Reading for Reflection:
    It is amazing how easily we can get lulled to sleep at times. I guess that's why so often the scriptures encourage us to stay awake and to wait in eager expectation, anticipating Christ's return at any moment. It is an actively passive waiting that's called for, if that's even possible. Like we talked about yesterday, we cannot control the *how* or the *where* or the *when* of his coming, so, in that sense, it must be passive. We can, however, control how we will wait for that coming. Therefore, it must also always be active. We must stay on our toes, or on our tiptoes, one might say. We must be on the edge of our seats, and not settled back into the comfort and ease of our La-Z-Boys. We must stay ready, both watching and waiting. That is the kind of wakefulness that is called for. We must keep our spiritual wits about us. We must be careful to do the things that keep our souls most awake and alert, whatever those things may be. Because, ultimately, Christ will come. And when he does, will he find us ready?

Closing Prayer: Most Holy God, awaken me from my soul's deep slumber and bring my life under your complete control. By your grace, awaken me daily to the reality of your presence within and around me. And, by the power of your Spirit, make me responsive to your will and your direction. Amen.

Thursday
First Week in Advent

Opening Prayer: Lord Jesus, prepare my heart for your coming. Work your work of grace deep within my soul and make me ready to receive you, my King. Amen.

Scripture Reading: Isaiah 40:1-5

Comfort, comfort my people,
    says your God.
Speak tenderly to Jerusalem,
    and proclaim to her
that her hard service has been completed,
    that her sin has been paid for,
that she has received from the Lord's hand
    double for all her sins.
A voice of one calling:
"In the wilderness prepare
    the way for the Lord;
make straight in the desert
    a highway for our God.
Every valley shall be raised up,
    every mountain and hill made low;
the rough ground shall become level,
    the rugged places a plain.
And the glory of the Lord will be revealed,
    and all people will see it together.
For the mouth of the Lord has spoken." (NIV)

Journal: What does it look like to prepare the way for the King to come into your heart?

What low places must be raised up?

What high places must be made low?

What rough places must be smoothed out?

And how will all of this preparation take place?

Reading for Reflection:

Do you ever catch yourself *trying too hard*? I caught myself doing that a couple of times recently. It is an interesting phenomenon. I'm not a hundred percent sure what happens, but somehow a situation, or a setting, bumps up against my insecurity and the next thing I know I'm either trying to be someone I'm not, or trying to be who I am on steroids — neither of which is a pretty sight.

And I'm not even sure most of the time whether the people I'm with can actually sense it or not, but I sure can. There is a neediness deep within me that rises to the surface and is impossible to escape or deny. A neediness that gives me one of two options: face it down and turn to God with it, or go with it and turn towards my own efforts, patterns, and devices. It definitely makes the words *"In returning and rest is your salvation; in quietness and trust is your strength. But you would have none of it"* (Isaiah 30:15) come to mind, and to life. It is only in turning — or returning — to God in the midst of the insecurity that I am able to face it and turn away from it, back toward God. Unfortunately, the couple of times I'm thinking about from my recent past didn't turn out quite the way I'd hoped.

Which brings me to our reading for the day (Isaiah 40:1-5). It is a passage about preparing the way for the entry of our God. It is a passage filled with all kinds of images of the construction and demolition that apparently are necessary parts of this preparation, removing the obstacles so that the King may arrive among us and within us. There is most assuredly work to be done — hard work. There are valleys — low places — that must be raised up. There are mountains — high places — that must be made low. There is rough ground that must be smoothed out. And there are rugged places that must become a plain.

And as I think about my *trying too hard*, I realize that there is much work to be done in me this season as well, as I prepare for the arrival of the King of Kings. The good news is that it is not all up to me. I am not left to face it on my own. It does not all depend on my efforts and my strength as I recognize what a mess I still am inside. It is God's work and as I turn (or return) to him, he will do the work in me. Mine is only to be open to his hand and to surrender to his Spirit and his will. He will do the work. He will free me from the compulsion of *trying too hard*. Whether it's trying to make an impression, or trying to win friends, or trying to be "the man," or whatever I might be *trying too hard* at the moment to achieve.

In the midst of my *trying too hard,* somehow, once again, I've forgotten the truth that my true (created in the image of God) self can never be created or achieved, it can only be received. So *trying too hard* is not just unfruitful, but also unnecessary. My job is to watch and wait, to pay attention, to recognize his voice and his Spirit, and allow him to do his work in me. And when I do this, then *the glory of the Lord will be revealed, and all people will see it together. For the mouth of the Lord has spoken.* Thanks be to God.

Closing Prayer: Lord God, prepare the ground of my soul for your coming. Give me the strength and the courage to recognize the work that needs to be done, to name it, and to be open to you as you *make straight a highway within me* for yourself. Come, Lord Jesus! Amen.

Friday
First Week in Advent

Opening Prayer: O Lord, my God, during this season of Advent, help me to wait for you eagerly and seek you earnestly. In the name of your Son and by the power of your Spirit I pray. Amen.

Scripture Reading: Isaiah 26:7-9

The path of the righteous is level;
  you make level the way of the righteous.
In the path of your judgments,
  O Lord, we wait for you;
your name and remembrance
  are the desire of our soul.
My soul yearns for you in the night;
  my spirit within me earnestly seeks you.
For when your judgments are in the earth,
  the inhabitants of the world learn righteousness. (ESV)

Journal: What is the true desire of your soul these days?

What do you yearn for most deeply?

What (or who) are you seeking earnestly?

What would it look like, during this season, to seek God before all else?

Reading for Reflection:

What does it look like to earnestly seek God? The dictionary tells us that the definition of the word *earnestly* is *"serious in intention, purpose, or effort; sincerely zealous."* Wow, that's a pretty weighty definition, particularly when we are applying it to our seeking of God. When I seek God, do I have serious intention, or is it just casual, haphazard, and random? Am I serious in purpose, or am I aimless and adrift? Am I serious in effort, or am I lackadaisical, tepid, and lazy? My guess is that if I indeed want to find Him in my seeking, it will depend a good bit on the earnestness of my seeking. At least that's what Jeremiah would tell us: *"You will seek me and find me, when you seek me with all your heart."* (Jeremiah 29:13)

The Hebrew word for *earnestly* is *shachar*, which means *"to seek diligently, or early."* This word gives the definite impression that the thing that is being sought in this manner is the first thing, the most important thing, or, as Jesus said, the *one thing*. When we seek something in this way <u>all</u> other things take a back seat. Thus, if *my soul* indeed *yearns for God in the night,* then the result of that yearning will be that *my spirit within me* will *earnestly seek* him.

So, back to the original question: What does it look like to earnestly seek God? Or, more specifically, what does it look like *for me* to earnestly seek God? And if I am not seeking him earnestly right now, exactly how am I seeking him? And is that enough? Is that enough for me? Is that enough for God? What am I earnestly seeking if it is not God? And what does that tell me? During this season, what will it take for me to make the leap from seeking him casually, or comfortably, or even routinely, to seeking him earnestly? And am I willing to make that leap?

Closing Prayer: O God, you are my God; earnestly I seek you; my soul thirsts for you; my flesh faints for you, as in a dry and weary land where there is no water. So I have looked upon you in the sanctuary, beholding your power and glory. Because your steadfast love is better than life, my lips will praise you. So I will bless you as long as I live; in your name I will lift up my hands. My soul will be satisfied as with fat and rich food, and my mouth will praise you with joyful lips, when I remember you upon my bed, and meditate on you in the watches of the night; for you have been my help, and in the shadow of your wings I will sing for joy. My soul clings to you; your right hand upholds me. (Psalm 63:1-8)

Saturday
First Week in Advent

Opening Prayer: Lord Jesus, help me to live my life fully convinced that you are coming back. And thus, help me to live in eager expectation and earnest longing for that day to arrive. And let that expectation and longing help me to determine what type of person I ought to be. Come, Lord Jesus! Amen.

Scripture Reading: 2 Peter 3:10-14

Yet it remains true that the day of the Lord will come as suddenly and unexpectedly as a thief. In that day the heavens will disappear in a terrific tearing blast, the very elements will disintegrate in heat and the earth and all that is in it will be burnt up to nothing.

In view of the fact that all these things are to be dissolved, what sort of people ought you to be? Surely men of good and holy character, who live expecting and earnestly longing for the coming of the day of God. True, this day will mean that the heavens will disappear in fire and the elements disintegrate in fearful heat, but our hopes are set not on these but on the new Heaven and the new earth which he has promised us, and in which nothing but good shall live.

Because, my dear friends, you have a hope like this before you, I urge you to make certain that such a day would find you at peace with God and man, clean and blameless in his sight. (JBP)

Journal: What kind of life do you long for Jesus to find you living when he returns?

How close to that is the life you are living today?

What will move you more fruitfully in the direction of the life you most deeply long to live?

Reading for Reflection:

Leave no doubt about it, *he will come.* He will come suddenly and unexpectedly, so we'd best be paying attention. During the season of Advent we do not just remember and celebrate the coming of God to a manger in Bethlehem, but we also remember and celebrate the fact that he will come again.

So, if we are wise, we will live with a sense of *eager expectation* and *earnest longing* for that day to come. So much so that it will have an impact on the way we live our lives. "If he is coming," Peter tells us, "we better be ready. We better be living the lives we think he would want us to be living."

What does that look like for you? In view of the fact that *he will come* — someday, somehow — into our world, what kind of people ought we *to be*? Notice that the question does not say, "What kind of things should we be *doing*?" as if we could somehow manufacture a behavior that would fool him into believing that our hearts are totally his. Instead, the question says, "What type of people ought we *to be*?" knowing that if he has captured our hearts, he will capture our behavior as well.

Being men and women of *good and holy character* is an inside job — it always flows from the inside out. We can't behave our way into holiness, it is impossible. We can only be captured into holiness. It starts with *being* in love with Jesus and then flows to *doing* whatever we think might please him, our Beloved. If we get this backwards we will be destined for a life of futility and frustration. Therefore, let us live lives of constant communion and intimacy with our beloved Jesus, knowing that when we do this we will always be eagerly looking forward to his arrival in our lives and in our world.

Closing Prayer: O Lord, since everything here today might well be gone tomorrow, help us to see how essential it is to live holy lives? Help us to live in daily expectation of the Day of the Lord, eagerly anticipating its arrival. And then, when that day finally comes, when the galaxies burn up and the elements melt down—help us to hardly notice. Help us to be looking not to what is burning up, but to what is being born—the promised new heavens and new earth, all beautifully adorned in your righteousness.

And since that is what we have to look forward to, O Lord, help us to do our best to be found living the lives you intended us to live when you dreamt us into being— lives of purity and of passion and of peace. Amen.

Second Sunday in Advent

Opening Prayer: O Christ Jesus, when all is darkness and we feel our weakness and helplessness, give us a sense of your presence, your love, and your strength. Help us to have perfect trust in your protecting love and strengthening power, so that nothing may frighten or worry us, for, living close to you, we shall see your hand, your purpose, your will through all things. ~St. Ignatius

Scripture Reading: John 11:32-44

Now when Mary came to where Jesus was and saw him, she fell at his feet, saying to him, "Lord, if you had been here, my brother would not have died." When Jesus saw her weeping, and the Jews who had come with her also weeping, he was deeply moved in his spirit and greatly troubled. And he said, "Where have you laid him?" They said to him, "Lord, come and see." Jesus wept. So the Jews said, "See how he loved him!" But some of them said, "Could not he who opened the eyes of the blind man also have kept this man from dying?"

Then Jesus, deeply moved again, came to the tomb. It was a cave, and a stone lay against it. Jesus said, "Take away the stone." Martha, the sister of the dead man, said to him, "Lord, by this time there will be an odor, for he has been dead four days." Jesus said to her, "Did I not tell you that if you believed you would see the glory of God?" So they took away the stone. And Jesus lifted up his eyes and said, "Father, I thank you that you have heard me. I knew that you always hear me, but I said this on account of the people standing around, that they may believe that you sent me." When he had said these things, he cried out with a loud voice, "Lazarus, come out." The man who had died came out, his hands and feet bound with linen strips, and his face wrapped with a cloth. Jesus said to them, "Unbind him, and let him go." (ESV)

Journal: Where have the circumstances of your life caused you to lose hope?

Where in your life are you finding it hard *to believe?*

What does the picture of a weeping God do within you?

Why do you think Jesus is weeping?

Do you believe that the pain in your life causes God's heart to break?

What would it look like for Jesus to stand with you in the deepest places of your pain?

Reading for Reflection:

The season of Advent is a season of hope. Hope that God will somehow show up amidst all of the chaos and turmoil and pain of this world. And, after watching a significant amount of pain in the last few weeks in the lives of several friends, I am coming to believe that *where we perceive God to be* in the midst of our chaos and pain is a very important thing. It determines so much about our process of healing, or at least it does for me.

Because in order to heal us, Jesus needs to get his hands on us. In order for us to find ourselves in his healing embrace, to hear his words of deep affection, and to allow his hands to tenderly mend our broken hearts, we have to be willing and open for that to occur. And that willingness and openness is largely determined by what we believe to be true about him; by where we think he is in the midst of our pain. Or, in other words, how we see him.

If we believe him to be distant or disinterested, or even the source and cause of our pain to begin with, we are unlikely to ever seek his healing touch. In that case we are more likely to feel abandoned or betrayed, which can become a source of anger and bitterness. But if we are able to believe that God is somehow mysteriously and wonderfully *with us* in the midst of our pain, that is a different story altogether. Then we are likely to have a deep sense of compassion *from* him and companionship *with* him. We are likely to realize that since he has experienced the depths of pain himself, he is wonderfully able to understand ours, and to truly be able to comfort us in the midst of it.

Thus, the season of Advent stands at the mysterious

intersection of groaning and hope. When we stand with Jesus at the tomb of Lazarus, seeing his tears and hearing his groans, we are likely to see the tears in his eyes and hear the groans of his heart over our pain as well. And then we can rest assured that even in the midst of our pain we are deeply known, deeply loved, and deeply understood. I don't know about you, but that gives birth to hope deep within me. Hope that I can, indeed, make it through *this,* whatever *this* may be. Hope that I am not alone to navigate it, but somehow more connected with him than I've ever been—more fertile to whatever he wants to plant within me and more receptive to the movement of his Spirit. Hope that somehow, someday I will be able to live again, not just surviving, but thriving because of the beauty he is able to bring out of my ashes. Now that's hope! Come, Lord Jesus!

Closing Prayer: Thank you, Lord Jesus that you wept. Thank you that you are a God who weeps—that our sorrow and sadness bring tears to your eyes as well. Thank you that you hold us, as well as all our tears, in the palm of your pierced hand. Amen.

Monday
Second Week in Advent

Opening Prayer: Lord, make me a channel of thy peace, that where there is hatred, I may bring love; that where there is wrong, I may bring the spirit of forgiveness; that where there is discord, I may bring harmony; that where there is error, I may bring truth; that where there is doubt, I may bring faith; that where there is despair, I may bring hope; that where there are shadows, I may bring light; that where there is sadness, I may bring joy. Lord, grant that I may seek rather to comfort than to be comforted; to understand, than to be understood; to love, than to be loved. For it is by self-forgetting that one finds. It is by forgiving that one is forgiven. It is by dying that one awakens to Eternal Life. ~ St. Francis of Assisi

Scripture Reading: Romans 8:19-29

For the creation waits with eager longing for the revealing of the sons of God. For the creation was subjected to futility, not willingly, but because of him who subjected it, in hope that the creation itself will be set free from its bondage to corruption and obtain the freedom of the glory of the children of God. For we know that the whole creation has been groaning together in the pains of childbirth until now. And not only the creation, but we ourselves, who have the firstfruits of the Spirit, groan inwardly as we wait eagerly for adoption as sons, the redemption of our bodies. For in this hope we were saved. Now hope that is seen is not hope. For who hopes for what he sees? But if we hope for what we do not see, we wait for it with patience.

Likewise the Spirit helps us in our weakness. For we do not know what to pray for as we ought, but the Spirit himself intercedes for us with groanings too deep for words. And he who searches hearts knows what is the mind of the Spirit, because the Spirit intercedes for the saints according to the will of God. And we know that for those who love God all things work together for good, for those who are called according to his purpose. (ESV)

Journal: What things cause groaning within you these days?

What things cause groaning around you?

How does it make you feel to know that God groans?

What does it do within you to know that the Spirit of God groans for you with *groanings too deep for words*?

Reading for Reflection:

Ultimately the season of Advent is a season of groaning; the groaning of our hearts and the groaning of our God. It is the groaning that comes from a deep longing for all to be as it was intended to be. Thus, it is a season where we fully recognize and embrace our sadness and frustration that all is not as it should be, rather than attempting to escape, avoid, or deny it. The world has gone terribly wrong, it is filled with decay and death, suffering and sadness, sorrow and pain; and yet, in the midst of it all, God meets us in a beautifully mysterious way. He meets us in a way in which we couldn't be met otherwise, making our groaning both a trust-filled embracing of where he has us, as well as a deep yearning for so much more—for deliverance and restoration, healing and wholeness.

Therefore, Advent is a season in which we watch and wait. It is a time in which we are filled with hope and with longing—hope that our Creator will finally intervene, and longing that he will enter into this world and set things aright once again, restoring all things to their creation intent.

Closing Prayer: May God the Father bless us, may Christ take care of us, may the Holy Spirit enlighten us all the days of our life. The Lord be our defender and keeper of body and soul, both now and for ever, to the ages of ages. Amen. ~ St. Ethelwold

Tuesday
Second Week in Advent

Opening Prayer: For you, O Lord, do I wait; it is you, O Lord my God, who will answer. (Psalm 38:15)

Scripture Reading: Romans 8:22-25

All around us we observe a pregnant creation. The difficult times of pain throughout the world are simply birth pangs. But it's not only around us; it's within us. The Spirit of God is arousing us within. We're also feeling the birth pangs. These sterile and barren bodies of ours are yearning for full deliverance. That is why waiting does not diminish us, any more than waiting diminishes a pregnant mother. We are enlarged in the waiting. We, of course, don't see what is enlarging us. But the longer we wait, the larger we become, and the more joyful our expectancy. (The Message)

Journal: What does the image of a pregnant creation do within you right now?

How does it make you hopeful?

How does it enlarge you?

How does it build a joyful expectancy?

Reading for Reflection:

o groaning
you wear many faces
today you are loneliness
yesterday you were longing
last week insecurity and inadequacy
and before that struggle, sadness, and pain

you are a constant companion
always present in one form or another
at times visible and recognizable
and at times hidden and buried deep within
so that i can hardly tell you are there

you walk with a purpose
opening up something deep inside me
creating fertile soil in my vulnerable heart
you expand my soul
hastening my becoming

you bring me low when i'm too high
make me smaller when i'm too big
you empty me of self when i'm too full of it
and meet me tenderly when i'm bruised or broken

you open me up
making me receptive to true presence
you accomplish a purpose
that only the Dreamer could possibly imagine

sometimes i run from you

sometimes i ignore you…or try
and sometimes i embrace you as a long lost friend
which is exactly what you are

o groaning
you wear many faces
work your work in me

Closing Prayer: Lord Jesus, we wait for you in the midst of this groaning world. Enlarge us, become larger in us, as we watch and wait for your coming. Build in us a joyful expectancy for your arrival. Come, Lord Jesus! Amen.

Wednesday
Second Week in Advent

Opening Prayer: When at last I cling to you with all my being, for me there will be no more sorrow, no more toil. Then at last I shall be alive with true life, for my life will be wholly filled by you. ~St. Augustine

Scripture Reading for the Day: Psalm 66:8-12

Praise our God, all peoples,
    let the sound of his praise be heard;
he has preserved our lives
    and kept our feet from slipping.
For you, God, tested us;
    you refined us like silver.
You brought us into prison
    and laid burdens on our backs.
You let people ride over our heads;
    we went through fire and water,
    but you brought us to a place of abundance. (NIV)

Journal: What are the places of struggle or challenge in your life right now?

How do you feel about those?

Where is God in the midst of them?

Where or how do you feel like you are being tested and refined?

Where or how do you feel like you have been led through fire and water?

Can you catch any glimpse of how this might lead to you being brought into a place of abundance?

What do you hope that looks like?

Reading for Reflection:

You *let* it happen, this *riding over our heads*, whoever or whatever that may have been. You didn't cause it, but you could have stopped it. I know it doesn't happen every day, but I have seen you spring into action and miraculously come to someone's aid or defense. I have seen you come to protect or deliver. And yet, for some reason, in this case, you didn't. You allowed *it*. Does that mean you sat idly by and watched? Or does it mean that—although the brokenness of this world was its cause—you are big enough to bring beauty out of the tragedy? You saw *it* coming, and *let* it stand, because of what you knew *it* would do within us. You knew that the groaning it would produce would have an effect on us like nothing else could or would.

So where exactly were you when we were going through the fire, being consumed by the agonizing flames of grief or sadness or mourning or pain? What were you doing while the mighty waters rushed over us and swept us away, as we struggled and fought to survive and keep our heads above water? Were you with us in some mysteriously hidden way that we were not able to completely comprehend at the time? Were you in the midst of the fire with us, shielding us from the fury of the flames? Were you in the middle of the raging currents beside us, holding and sustaining us—keeping us afloat? After all, you know what the groaning is like; in fact, you know it like no other. Did it break your heart to have to watch this *riding over us* unfold; to know the depths of the pain we were going through, and not intervene? How hard that must have been for you.

When we are in the midst of *the groan* it is hellish. It is hard to believe, or even consent to the fact, that something good might possibly result from the chaos and brokenness. Much less to think that it could be some strange path to a place called *abundance*. That is almost unthinkable. Yet all of us, on the backside of this *riding over*, usually have to admit that something took place within us—or among us—that could have happened no other way. We would never have chosen the path in a million years—not then, and most likely not again—but we can't deny the beauty of the new place where we eventually arrived. How in the world did we get there? Who would've imagined that the groans and cries and tears and struggle would have brought us to that place; that place where our hearts were both broken and expanded, where our souls were both crushed and deepened beyond measure. Who could've dreamt that the effect of the fire and the water would have been to make us more like Jesus—he who *suffers with* and delivers, he who *weeps over* and heals?

There has been a lot of groaning going around lately. It seems to be coming from every direction. I guess it is true that "each one of us sits beside a pool of tears." And it is so hard to watch the groaners groan and the mourners mourn and the strugglers struggle and not be able to do anything but pray. It is so tempting to try and come to the rescue, but rescue is not really possible, or even preferable. Because something much deeper is going on. In the words of Gerald May, "There is no way out, only through." Something deep and wonderful happens in the *going through*. So we must resist the urge to provide an escape— if that were even possible—because the struggle, or the groaning, or the grief, or the pain is the very thing that is able to do a beautiful work within us. All there is for us to do is trust. Trust that God really is in control. Trust that God really is up to something, in spite of all appearances. Trust that God really is big enough to sustain, to comfort, to deliver, to heal, and ultimately to transform. Trust that through the fire and through the water lies *a place of abundance.*

Closing Prayer: Bless our God, O peoples! Give him a thunderous welcome! Didn't he set us on the road to life? Didn't he keep us out of the ditch? He trained us first, passed us like silver through refining fires, brought us into hardscrabble country, pushed us to our very limit, road-tested us inside and out, took us to hell and back; finally he brought us to this well-watered place. (Psalm 66:8-12, *The Message*)

Thursday
Second Week in Advent

Opening Prayer: O God, help us to live these days and weeks with the holy expectation that you will show up. Help us to never get so lulled to sleep by our daily rituals and routines that we miss you right in the midst of our everyday lives. Come to us, O Lord, and bring something new to life within us. Amen.

Scripture Reading: Luke 1:5-25

In the time of Herod king of Judea there was a priest named Zechariah, who belonged to the priestly division of Abijah; his wife Elizabeth was also a descendant of Aaron. Both of them were righteous in the sight of God, observing all the Lord's commands and decrees blamelessly. But they were childless because Elizabeth was not able to conceive, and they were both very old.

Once when Zechariah's division was on duty and he was serving as priest before God, he was chosen by lot, according to the custom of the priesthood, to go into the temple of the Lord and burn incense. And when the time for the burning of incense came, all the assembled worshipers were praying outside.

Then an angel of the Lord appeared to him, standing at the right side of the altar of incense. When Zechariah saw him, he was startled and was gripped with fear. But the angel said to him: "Do not be afraid, Zechariah; your prayer has been heard. Your wife Elizabeth will bear you a son, and you are to call him John. He will be a joy and delight to you, and many will rejoice because of his birth, for he will be great in the sight of the Lord.

He is never to take wine or other fermented drink, and he will be filled with the Holy Spirit even before he is born. He will bring back many of the people of Israel to the Lord their God. And he will go on before the Lord, in the spirit and power of Elijah, to turn the hearts of the parents to their children and the disobedient to the wisdom of the righteous – to make ready a people prepared for the Lord."

Zechariah asked the angel, "How can I be sure of this? I am an old man and my wife is well along in years."

The angel said to him, "I am Gabriel. I stand in the presence of God, and I have been sent to speak to you and to tell you this good news. And now you will be silent and not able to speak until the day this happens, because you did not believe my words, which will come true at their appointed time."

Meanwhile, the people were waiting for Zechariah and wondering why he stayed so long in the temple. When he came out, he could not speak to them. They realized he had seen a vision in the temple, for he kept making signs to them but remained unable to speak.

When his time of service was completed, he returned home. After this his wife Elizabeth became pregnant and for five months remained in seclusion. "The Lord has done this for me," *she said. "In these days he has shown his favor and taken away my disgrace among the people." (NIV)*

Journal: In what ways are you longing for God to show up like he did for Zechariah?

What are you longing for him to do in you, or for you?

Where in your life are you asking the question, "How can I be sure of this?"

And in what ways do you feel like Elizabeth?

Why do you think silence was a part of the experience for both of them?

What happened in the silence?

Reading for Reflection:

Our lives are full. Oh, maybe not full in the qualitative sense (as in *all the fullness of God - Eph. 3:19*), but full of other, not so quality things. We are full of doubt, full of fear, and full of insecurity. We are full of activities, full of responsibilities, and full of stuff to do. We are full of disappointment, full of groaning, and full of pain. We are full of distractions, full of expectations, and full of demands. We are simply full! And if we are totally honest, the biggest thing we are full of is ourselves. No wonder there are so few times when we actually feel full of God. How could we? We are so full of other things that there is simply no room. An *emptying* must take place in order for any new kind of filling to be possible.

Elizabeth was full of disgrace. She had lived for so many years being called "barren." What an awful thing to be called. Look at some of the definitions of that word: *not producing or incapable of producing offspring; sterile: unproductive; unfruitful: without capacity to interest or attract.* The Greek word used here is *steira*, which means *hard, stiff, or unnatural.* For a Jewish woman, in her time and place, I'm guessing it was not the kind of word she wanted to be known by. It was not a name she wanted to be called. It was a name that pointed out her inabilities as a woman. And so Elizabeth, because she was *barren,* was filled with *disgrace.*

But God was about to change all of that. He was about to take away, or *empty* her of, all that disgrace and fill her instead with his *favor.* What a great word. God was about to fill Elizabeth, not only with the child she most deeply longed for, but with something much, much more — his *favor.*

So God birthed something new deep in her body, as well as her soul, and she was completely overwhelmed. So much so that she had to ponder all of this, she had to take time and reflect on the magnitude of what had happened to her, in order to nurture this new birth that had just taken place within her — both physically and spiritually. So instead of running around showing everyone that God had *taken away her disgrace*, she went into seclusion for five months. She immediately went into silence, where she knew this new birth could best be cared for, nurtured, and grown before it was ready to be seen by the world. I wonder what those five months were like for her. And I wonder if she was a totally different person when the time in silence was complete. She had received a gift from God and had to make it her own before it would be of any value to anyone else.

I'm really drawn to Elizabeth during this season. I'm drawn to her emptying and to her filling. I'm drawn to the silence she goes into in order to nurture this new life of God within her. Elizabeth is such a great guide for us during Advent. What emptying needs to take place in us? What new life does God long to plant within us? How will we pay attention to and care for and nurture this life in order to allow it the space and the time to become all that God desires it to be?

Closing Prayer: O Lord my God, help me to wait for you and to never lose heart. Help me to hold on to the assurance and confidence that, in your own time and in your own way, you will come to me and conceive some new life deep within me. Amen.

Friday
Second Week in Advent

Opening Prayer: Yes, Father! Yes! And always Yes!
~Francis de Sales

Scripture Reading: Luke 1:26-38

In the sixth month of Elizabeth's pregnancy, God sent the angel Gabriel to Nazareth, a town in Galilee, to a virgin pledged to be married to a man named Joseph, a descendant of David. The virgin's name was Mary. The angel went to her and said, "Greetings, you who are highly favored! The Lord is with you."

Mary was greatly troubled at his words and wondered what kind of greeting this might be. But the angel said to her, "Do not be afraid, Mary; you have found favor with God. You will conceive and give birth to a son, and you are to call him Jesus. He will be great and will be called the Son of the Most High. The Lord God will give him the throne of his father David, and he will reign over Jacob's descendants forever; his kingdom will never end."

"How will this be," Mary asked the angel, "since I am a virgin?"

The angel answered, "The Holy Spirit will come on you, and the power of the Most High will overshadow you. So the holy one to be born will be called the Son of God. Even Elizabeth your relative is going to have a child in her old age, and she who was said to be unable to conceive is in her sixth month. For no word from God will ever fail."

"I am the Lord's servant," Mary answered. "May your word to me be fulfilled." Then the angel left her. (NIV)

Journal: How do you imagine this scene unfolding? Put yourself in Mary's shoes and imagine what it would have been like to have had this conversation with Gabriel. For the next few minutes try to take on her posture. Hold yourself open before God in prayer. After you have finished that exercise, write down your response in the space that follows.

Reading for Reflection:

Don't you wish sometimes that you could've been a fly on the wall as these great stories of Scripture unfolded? Especially one like this. I would have loved to have seen the faces of Mary and Gabriel as this exchange took place. I would have loved to have heard the words, to have heard how they were spoken and with what tone and care and volume. And I would have loved to have seen how those words were received. What did it look like when Mary was *greatly troubled* (disturbed) by the words, even in the midst of being filled with wonder about what they might mean and how they would be fulfilled? I'm guessing that she was incredibly excited about the amazing thing God was getting ready to do, but troubled by what it might mean for her life, her heart, and her family. I sort of get it. I've had somewhat similar feelings before. I've sensed God's invitation to do an incredibly intimate work deep within me and been so excited about it, but afraid of it all at the same time. I mean the Holy Spirit was going to *come upon* her, the Most High God was going to *overshadow* her. And the result was going to be that God himself would somehow be conceived within her.

And you have to love Mary's response. After all, God was asking something that was incredibly demanding of her — total openness. She was to completely *hold herself open* to him; totally vulnerable, totally willing, totally receptive to whatever he might choose to do. It is a frightening posture to hold, unless the one that you hold it for is utterly loving and trustworthy. Then, and only then, are we able to respond as she did: *"Behold, I am the servant of the Lord; let it be to me according to your word."*

I have a suspicion that the Spirit of the Most High would like to do something unspeakably intimate within each of us as well, something that will fill us with joyful wonder and greatly disturb us all at the same time. And if we have the courage to *hold ourselves open* to him (willing, receptive, and vulnerable) and if we have the courage to answer him with the words of Mary ("*I am the servant of the Lord; let it be to me according to your word.*") then he will *come upon* us as well and *overshadow* us and birth himself in us in an indescribably intimate way — which is, in fact, the deepest desire of our hearts. Come, Lord Jesus! Thanks be to God!

Closing Prayer: Lord God, I belong to you, body and soul. I am your servant. Let it be unto me according to your word. Amen.

Saturday
Second Week in Advent

Opening Prayer: O living flame of love that tenderly wounds my soul in its deepest center! Since now you are not oppressive, now consummate! If it be your will: tear through the veil of this sweet encounter!

O sweet cautery, O delightful wound! O gentle hand! O delicate touch that tastes of eternal life and pays every debt! In killing you changed death to life.

O lamps of fire! In whose splendors the deep caverns of feeling, once obscure and blind, now give forth, so rarely, so exquisitely, both warmth and light to their Beloved.

How gently and lovingly you wake in my heart, where in secret you dwell alone; and in your sweet breathing, filled with good and glory, how tenderly you swell my heart with love. ~John of the Cross

Scripture Reading: Luke 1:35

"The Holy Spirit will come on you, and the power of the Most High will overshadow you. So the holy one to be born will be called the Son of God." (NIV)

Journal: Imagine what this encounter between Mary and the Holy Spirit must've been like. Imagine the passion. Imagine the intimacy. Realize that God wants passionate, intimate union with you as well. Sit for a few minutes in the silent embrace of the Lover of your soul. Afterwards, write about that experience in the space that follows.

Reading for Reflection:

What exactly happened in that moment? That wonder-filled instant when the Holy Spirit *came upon* you, when the Most High *overshadowed* you? What was it like? I have to know! Was it heavenly? Was it more wonderful than anything you ever dreamed of, or dared to imagine? God *entered into* you, he penetrated you to the core, more deeply than anyone ever thought possible. God, the Most High, *entered into* you, and that entry created new life. He left something of his life-giving-self inside, something beautiful beyond imagination was conceived in you. You were pregnant with God and had the unbelievable privilege of carrying him around inside of you; of nurturing his new life within you until time reached its fullness and he was ready to come forth, to show himself, to be born into this world. You, Mary, are the *theotokos* — the God-bearer, because God *entered into* you.

And because he *entered into* you, he can *enter into* us as well. May we, too, be open to the unspeakable intimacy of that entry. May we, too, allow ourselves to be *overshadowed* by you, the Most High God. May you *enter into* us, penetrate us to the core, and bring to life something of yourself deep within our souls. May we, too, be pregnant with God, and nurture and care for his new life within us until it is ready to be born into our lives, born into our world.

Closing Prayer: Listen to God's words of affection for you: *You, my Beloved, have captured my heart. I am filled to overflowing with affection for you. O give me now your heart, lest mine burst within me. One second more I cannot stand* *without the company of your presence, without the warmth of your embrace. I think about you all the hours of the day, yearning for your glance, your smile, your touch. I am totally captivated by you! O how I long for you to know the depths of my affection and the wild intensity of my passionate love. I love you, O my Beloved. You are mine.*

Third Sunday in Advent

Opening Prayer: God, of thy goodness, give me Thyself; for Thou art enough for me, and I can ask for nothing less that can be full honor to Thee. And if I ask anything that is less, ever shall I be in want, for only in Thee have I all. ~Julian of Norwich

Scripture Reading: Luke 1:39-56

And Mary said,

"My soul magnifies the Lord,
*   and my spirit rejoices in God my Savior,*
for he has looked on the humble estate of his servant.
*   For behold, from now on all generations will call me blessed;*
for he who is mighty has done great things for me,
*   and holy is his name.*
And his mercy is for those who fear him
*   from generation to generation.*
He has shown strength with his arm;
*   he has scattered the proud in the thoughts of their hearts;*
he has brought down the mighty from their thrones
*   and exalted those of humble estate;*
he has filled the hungry with good things,
*   and the rich he has sent away empty.*
He has helped his servant Israel,
*   in remembrance of his mercy,*
as he spoke to our fathers,
*   to Abraham and to his offspring forever."*

And Mary remained with her about three months and returned to her home. (ESV)

Journal: What song is your soul singing these days? Write your song of thanksgiving and celebration to God today. How will you magnify him?

Reading for Reflection:

Magnificat. It is a Latin word which means *magnifies.* It is also the name by which this prayer of Mary's has been known throughout the ages. It is truly one of the great prayers of all time. It is the prayer of an innocent and obedient young girl who decided to say *yes* to God, even in the most overwhelming, challenging, and ridiculous of circumstances. It is a prayer of trust. It is a prayer of surrender. But most of all it is a prayer of total openness. It is a prayer that reveals a heart that is held wide open to whatever God might desire and to however he might choose to show up. It is a prayer that literally says, *Come, Lord Jesus! Come to us. Come among us. Come be born in us.*

Therefore, it is also a prayer of invitation. And if we too desire God to be born in us this day, and in this season, maybe it is a prayer we should pay attention to. Because, for God to be born in us, a certain posture seems to be required. It seems that God has a preference for the lowly, the vulnerable, and the small. It is in those kinds of places among those kinds of people that he seems most likely to be born.

Just look at the prayer: *My soul magnifies the Lord, and my spirit rejoices in God my Savior, for he has looked on the humble estate of his servant.* And then a little later: *he has brought down the mighty from their thrones and exalted those of humble estate.* The word used here for *humble* comes from the root *tapeinos* which means "to make low." Somehow Mary's *low estate* provided the perfect womb (soul) in which God could be born. Somehow there was room in that kind of soul; room that is typically filled in those of us that are full of ourselves. Filled with our pride and our ambition and our reputation. It seems that the *proud,* the *rulers,* and the *rich* have a difficult time making space within themselves for this to birth to occur.

Therefore, may we never become too big, or too high, or too occupied to miss how Jesus wants to come to us this season—how he wants to be born in us. May we pray this incredible prayer, both in word and in spirit, with Mary, that our hearts might be open and prepared to receive him, whenever and however he comes.

Closing Prayer: I'm bursting with God-news; I'm dancing the song of my Savior God. God took one good look at me, and look what happened—I'm the most fortunate woman on earth! What God has done for me will never be forgotten, the God whose very name is holy, set apart from all others. His mercy flows in wave after wave on those who are in awe before him. He bared his arm and showed his strength, scattered the bluffing braggarts. He knocked tyrants off their high horses, pulled victims out of the mud. The starving poor sat down to a banquet; the callous rich were left out in the cold. He embraced his chosen child, Israel; he remembered and piled on the mercies, piled them high. It's exactly what he promised, beginning with Abraham and right up to now. (Luke 1:46-55, *The Message*)

Monday
Third Week in Advent

Opening Prayer: O God of promise, we wait in hope for the fulfillment of all the things you have said will one day come to pass, both within us and around us. Give us unfailing confidence in your character, unlimited trust in your heart, and undying gratitude when we finally receive that which you have promised. Amen.

Scripture Reading: Luke 1:57-80

Now the time came for Elizabeth to give birth, and she bore a son. And her neighbors and relatives heard that the Lord had shown great mercy to her, and they rejoiced with her. And on the eighth day they came to circumcise the child. And they would have called him Zechariah after his father, but his mother answered, "No; he shall be called John." And they said to her, "None of your relatives is called by this name." And they made signs to his father, inquiring what he wanted him to be called. And he asked for a writing tablet and wrote, "His name is John." And they all wondered. And immediately his mouth was opened and his tongue loosed, and he spoke, blessing God. And fear came on all their neighbors. And all these things were talked about through all the hill country of Judea, and all who heard them laid them up in their hearts, saying, "What then will this child be?" For the hand of the Lord was with him.

And his father Zechariah was filled with the Holy Spirit and prophesied, saying,

"Blessed be the Lord God of Israel,
    for he has visited and redeemed his people
and has raised up a horn of salvation for us
    in the house of his servant David,
as he spoke by the mouth of his holy prophets from of old,
that we should be saved from our enemies
    and from the hand of all who hate us;
to show the mercy promised to our fathers
    and to remember his holy covenant,
the oath that he swore to our father Abraham, to grant us
    that we, being delivered from the hand of our enemies,
might serve him without fear,
    in holiness and righteousness before him all our days.
And you, child, will be called the prophet of the Most High;
    for you will go before the Lord to prepare his ways,
to give knowledge of salvation to his people
    in the forgiveness of their sins,
because of the tender mercy of our God,
    whereby the sunrise shall visit us from on high
to give light to those who sit in darkness and in the shadow of
death, to guide our feet into the way of peace."

    And the child grew and became strong in spirit, and he was in
the wilderness until the day of his public appearance to Israel.
(ESV)

Journal: Can you relate to Zechariah and Elizabeth? How?

Has there ever been a time when you received something you were desperately praying for and hoping for?

What was that like?

What did it produce within you?

Is there some way or some place in your life you are still waiting for God to show up?

How do you feel about that?

Reading for Reflection:

What actually happens in the garden of *waiting?* What kind of fruit is produced in its soil? Whatever it is, it must be breathtakingly beautiful, particularly given how often the scriptures call upon us to abide there. It definitely gives you the impression that whatever *it* is that is being waited for is not ultimately the only good thing to be received. We also receive the *fruit* of the process. That is probably the reason it takes so much time and attention for a tiny seed to grow into a beautiful flower. Something is produced in the waiting and the watering and the tending that would not be produced otherwise — patience, trust, gratitude, and appreciation.

You have to wonder if that was not at least a part of the reason God required Zechariah and Elizabeth to wait so long. They had waited years to bear children to begin with, and finally God showed up in a rather remarkable way and answered their prayers. But then there was the whole nine months of waiting for their baby to arrive — it must've felt like an eternity. But again, God was up to something in their waiting. While he was growing a child in Elizabeth's womb, he was also growing his good fruit in the soil of their souls.

You need look no further than Zechariah's prayer to see abundant evidence of it. It is a prayer blooming with the fruit of thanksgiving, gratitude, and appreciation. If ever there were two parents who would not take the gift of a child for granted, it was these two. They knew that John (or *Ioannes* in the Greek, which means *Jehovah is a gracious giver*) was a true gift from God, and they would treat him that way all the days of his life. Something beautiful had grown in their souls through waiting that enabled them to truly appreciate and understand the great gift they were being given.

Closing Prayer: Blessed be the Lord, the God of Israel; he came and set his people free. He set the power of salvation in the center of our lives, and in the very house of David his servant, just as he promised long ago through the preaching of his holy prophets: Deliverance from our enemies and every hateful hand; mercy to our fathers, as he remembers to do what he said he'd do, what he swore to our father Abraham — a clean rescue from the enemy camp, so we can worship him without a care in the world, made holy before him as long as we live. And you, my child, "Prophet of the Highest," will go ahead of the Master to prepare his ways, present the offer of salvation to his people, the forgiveness of their sins. Through the heartfelt mercies of our God, God's Sunrise will break in upon us, shining on those in the darkness, those sitting in the shadow of death, then showing us the way, one foot at a time, down the path of peace. (Luke 1:67-79, *The Message*)

Tuesday
Third Week in Advent

Opening Prayer: O God, sometimes you ask us to do the impossible; you ask us to trust you even when things are beyond our understanding or comprehension. Help us to have the courage and the faith to do so, to trust you even in the midst of the most chaotic and trying and difficult circumstances of our lives. Amen.

Scripture Reading: Matthew 1:18-25

Now the birth of Jesus Christ took place in this way. When his mother Mary had been betrothed to Joseph, before they came together she was found to be with child from the Holy Spirit. And her husband Joseph, being a just man and unwilling to put her to shame, resolved to divorce her quietly. But as he considered these things, behold, an angel of the Lord appeared to him in a dream, saying, "Joseph, son of David, do not fear to take Mary as your wife, for that which is conceived in her is from the Holy Spirit. She will bear a son, and you shall call his name Jesus, for he will save his people from their sins." All this took place to fulfill what the Lord had spoken by the prophet:

"Behold, the virgin shall conceive and bear a son, and they shall call his name Immanuel"

(which means, God with us). When Joseph woke from sleep, he did as the angel of the Lord commanded him: he took his wife, but knew her not until she had given birth to a son. And he called his name Jesus. (ESV)

Journal: How would you have felt if you were Joseph?

What would you have been tempted to do?

What circumstances in your life right now are requiring you to trust God completely?

Reading for Reflection:

I wonder how long you made Joseph wait in that agonizing tension before you told him your plan. And what was it you were trying to accomplish within him in the midst of his struggling and wrestling? Were you trying to teach him to pray? Were you building his character? Were you testing his faith? Were you trying to see if he would say *yes* to you regardless of the situation or circumstances? Were you increasing his groaning, because you knew it would make the soil of his soul fertile and receptive to your coming? Was the time of struggle designed to increase the depths of his gratitude once you finally told him the truth? Was it to test his love for Mary, the mother of your Son? Was it to test his love for you? What was that awful, struggle-filled waiting meant to do in him? And what is it meant to do in *me*? How am I, like Joseph, looking at a seemingly no-win situation and having to trust you to somehow show up in the middle of it? Where am I watching and waiting and trusting you to help me begin to make sense of it all? Where am I *waiting* desperately for you to arrive? Come, Lord Jesus!

Closing Prayer: Lord God, help us to trust you even in the midst of our waiting and uncertainty, that through it all we may remain certain of one thing—you! Amen.

Wednesday
Third Week in Advent

Opening Prayer: O Great Light of the world, illuminate our darkness and fill us with the light of life. Amen.

Scripture Reading: John 1:4-13

In him was life, and that life was the light of all mankind. The light shines in the darkness, and the darkness has not overcome it.

There was a man sent from God whose name was John. He came as a witness to testify concerning that light, so that through him all might believe. He himself was not the light; he came only as a witness to the light.

The true light that gives light to everyone was coming into the world. He was in the world, and though the world was made through him, the world did not recognize him. He came to that which was his own, but his own did not receive him. Yet to all who did receive him, to those who believed in his name, he gave the right to become children of God – children born not of natural descent, nor of human decision or a husband's will, but born of God. (NIV)

Journal: Where is there darkness within you?

What form does it typically take?

What would it look like for Jesus to come into that darkness?

Reading for Reflection:
This season always causes me to think a lot about darkness and light. In fact, it usually causes me to become more keenly aware of the darkness that lives within me, which often takes the form of fear, insecurity, anxiety, and depression. It can quickly take me right down into the pit of despair, and it is so deep at times that it actually seems like a part of my DNA. In fact, when it takes hold of me it seems almost impossible to overcome its grip, much less consider even the possibility of being free of it completely, which can leave me in a very dark and helpless place.

I think that's one of the reasons I like Advent so much, because it's a season of hope. Advent promises that it is actually *into* the midst of my darkness that the light *will* come. I do not have to eliminate the darkness within me—which seems an impossible task anyway—all I have to do is simply watch and wait for the coming of the Light. He *will* come, and when he does the darkness will not be able to overcome him. So shine on me, O Light. Come into my darkness and illumine my night with your life and love and peace. Come, O Light of God! Come, Lord Jesus!

Closing Prayer: Shine on me, O Light. Come into my darkness and illumine my night with your life and love and peace. Come, O Light of God! Come, Lord Jesus!

Thursday
Third Week in Advent

Opening Prayer: O Most Holy God, how can we possibly prepare for your coming? You are the Holy One and require those who come before you to be the same. Thank you, Lord God, that you sent Jesus to consecrate us with his blood and to wash us with his righteousness, that we may stand before you holy and blameless when you finally choose to come again. Help us to hold fast to Jesus, our righteousness. Amen.

Scripture Reading: Exodus 19:10-11

When Moses told the words of the people to the Lord, the Lord said to Moses, "Go to the people and consecrate them today and tomorrow, and let them wash their garments and be ready for the third day. For on the third day the Lord will come down on Mount Sinai in the sight of all the people." (NIV)

Journal: What do the words to Exodus 19:10-11 do within you?

How will you prepare for his coming?

Reading for Reflection:

"Are you ready for Christmas?" It is funny this time of year how many times a day you are asked that question. And I don't know about you, but the minute I hear it my mind goes immediately to whether I have bought all of my presents, or if the lights are up, or the tree is up, or if I have done the million-and-one other things that *must* be done before Christmas Day arrives. Getting ready for Christmas can be a bit overwhelming at times, but I wonder if there is not a deeper call I need to hear in that question. What if being ready for Christmas has more to do with *being prepared,* which seems to have much more to do with the state of my heart and soul than it does the state of my Christmas *to do* list?

Isaiah knew what I'm talking about: *A voice cries: "In the wilderness prepare the way of the Lord; make straight in the desert a highway for our God. Every valley shall be lifted up, and every mountain and hill be made low; the uneven ground shall become level, and the rough places a plain. And the glory of the Lord shall be revealed, and all flesh shall see it together, for the mouth of the Lord has spoken."* (Isaiah 40:3-5) There is a certain amount of preparing that needs to be done when the God of all creation is about to enter that very creation. And it has much more to do with what is going on within us than it does about what is going on around us. There is much work to do *within* before God arrives. Valleys must be raised up. Mountains and hills must be made low. The uneven ground of our hearts and souls must be made level, and the rough places smoothed into a plain. After all, the King is coming. Let us prepare the way for him.

It is easy to get lost in the visions of mangers and

shepherds and angels and stars and babes in swaddling clothes and forget that this tiny baby, born in Bethlehem, is both the King of Kings and the Lord of Lords. It is easy to allow ourselves to be filled with wonder and amazement about the beauty breaking in within us and around us and miss the awe and the reverence (and even terror) of realizing that a holy God is about to enter our world. So maybe I should spend some time, like God directed Moses, doing some serious preparing *within* before he arrives. Maybe I too need to turn my mind and my heart to the ways I need to be cleansed and consecrated before he appears. The word *consecrate* comes from the Hebrew word *qadash* which is a verb meaning to sanctify, to be holy, to separate, to set apart, or to be pure and clean. God tells Moses to make sure the people of Israel have prepared themselves in this way for his coming. *Wash your garments, and your hearts, because a holy God is coming down out of the heavens to descend on Mount Sinai. Therefore, be it Sinai or Bethlehem, get ready.*

Which makes me ask myself, "Am I really ready for Christmas?" If Advent is about watching and waiting for his coming, shouldn't I be doing the same? Shouldn't I spend the days and weeks of Advent consecrating and cleansing, preparing myself for the arrival of my awesome and holy God? And what does that even look like for me? God, how do you want me to prepare for your arrival?

So I guess tomorrow, when the next person asks me if I'm ready for Christmas, I think my reply will have to be, "*Probably not. I've still got some preparing to do.*"

God said to Moses, "Go to the people. For the next two days get these people ready to meet the Holy God. Have them scrub their clothes so that on the third day they'll be fully prepared, because on the third day God will come down on Mount Sinai and make his presence known to all the people." (Exodus 19:10-11, The Message)

Closing Prayer: Make me holy, O Lord, wholly yours, for you will not accept any less than all of me. Amen.

Friday
Third Week in Advent

Opening Prayer: O Lord my God, you are a consuming fire. Keep my lamp ever-burning with passionate love for you, that I might be ready for you when you return for the wedding feast. Amen.

Scripture Reading: Luke 12:35-40

"Be dressed ready for service and keep your lamps burning, like servants waiting for their master to return from a wedding banquet, so that when he comes and knocks they can immediately open the door for him. It will be good for those servants whose master finds them watching when he comes. Truly I tell you, he will dress himself to serve, will have them recline at the table and will come and wait on them. It will be good for those servants whose master finds them ready, even if he comes in the middle of the night or toward daybreak. But understand this: If the owner of the house had known at what hour the thief was coming, he would not have let his house be broken into. You also must be ready, because the Son of Man will come at an hour when you do not expect him." (NIV)

Journal: What is the state of your *lamp* these days?

What is burning within you?

Are you burning with the fires of the Spirit?

What things in your life or practice help fan those flames?

What hinders them?

How will you tend your inner fires during this season?

Reading for Reflection:
Cast aside everything that might extinguish this small flame
which is beginning to burn within you, and surround yourself
with everything which can feed and fan it into a stronger flame.
(The Art of Prayer)

There is a flame within us, started and sustained by
God's Spirit, that we are required to tend. It is the part of
us that burns for God, for intimacy with him, and for his
Kingdom to be revealed in this world. In some this fire is a
raging inferno. In fact, it is so real and so present that if
you get within a certain proximity of these people you will
be warmed by the heat of its passion. And in others this
fire is weak and smoldering, like a dim wick that is on the
verge of being snuffed out completely. It is of no use to
anyone.

And though we cannot control the source of this fire, we
are called to tend and feed and fan its flame. We are called
to make sure to *keep our lamps burning.* Therefore, we must
be thoughtful and intentional as we consider how to
nurture and stoke this fire within us. We must learn to
listen and reflect and pray in a way that allows us to see
how to create the proper conditions for this fire to thrive,
and for its flames to grow. We must regularly ask
ourselves certain questions like: "What are the things that
keep my inner fires going? When and how will I make
those things a regular part of my life? What fuels my soul
to keep me stumbling toward love? Who are the people
and what are the practices that ignite something deep
within me?" And when we finally begin to get a sense of
the answers to some of these questions, we need to go to

work, to start gathering those logs and tossing them on the fire.

Closing Prayer: O living flame of love that tenderly wounds my soul in its deepest center! Since now you are not oppressive, now consummate! If it be your will: tear through the veil of this sweet encounter! O sweet cautery, O delightful wound! O gentle hand! O delicate touch that tastes of eternal life and pays every debt! In killing you changed death to life. O lamps of fire! In whose splendors the deep caverns of feeling, once obscure and blind, now give forth, so rarely, so exquisitely, both warmth and light to their Beloved. How gently and lovingly you wake in my heart, where in secret you dwell alone; and in your sweet breathing, filled with good and glory, how tenderly you swell my heart with love. ~John of the Cross

Saturday
Third Week in Advent

Opening Prayer: O great God of Life, begin a new work of life and love deep within me this day. Amen.

Scripture Reading: Isaiah 42:1-9

"Here is my servant, whom I uphold,
*   my chosen one in whom I delight;*
I will put my Spirit on him,
*   and he will bring justice to the nations.*
He will not shout or cry out,
*   or raise his voice in the streets.*
A bruised reed he will not break,
*   and a smoldering wick he will not snuff out.*
In faithfulness he will bring forth justice;
*   he will not falter or be discouraged*
till he establishes justice on earth.
*   In his teaching the islands will put their hope."*
This is what God the Lord says —
the Creator of the heavens, who stretches them out,
*   who spreads out the earth with all that springs from it,*
*   who gives breath to its people,*
*   and life to those who walk on it:*
"I, the Lord, have called you in righteousness;
*   I will take hold of your hand.*
I will keep you and will make you
*   to be a covenant for the people*
*   and a light for the Gentiles,*
to open eyes that are blind,

to free captives from prison
and to release from the dungeon those who sit in darkness.
"I am the Lord; that is my name!
I will not yield my glory to another
or my praise to idols.
See, the former things have taken place,
and new things I declare;
before they spring into being
I announce them to you." (NIV)

Journal: Where and how do you long to be made new?

What new work do you desire God to do in you?

Reading for Reflection:

New is something we all deeply long for. In fact, which one of us is not excited about a new beginning, or a clean slate, or a new lease on life, or a brand new heart? Who among us is not thrilled at the prospect of all that is old and worn out and broken-down being done away with in favor of what is new and fresh and whole? But I'll be the first to admit that as much as I yearn for all things to be made new, I don't want it to cost me too much. I don't want it to be a process that is slow and difficult, arduous and long. I want it to just suddenly appear, to be as quick and as easy as possible — like waving some sort of magic wand.

New birth, however, does not come easy. In fact, the birthing process is often a long and painful one. I guess that's why it's called *labor*. And the necessity of this *labor* is not only true of physical birth, but of spiritual birth as well. That does not mean that we can somehow work our way into some new state of being or of seeing. The new thing, whatever it may be, must be *conceived* in us, and that is something that we ultimately have no control over; no more control than Mary had as the Spirit *came upon her*.

The *birthing* of this new thing, however, is a different story altogether. The birthing process, the process of bringing this *new thing* into existence, requires a labor — a labor that is likely filled with much pain and turmoil and struggle. A pain and a turmoil and a struggle that is offset, however, by the overwhelming joy of seeing this *new thing* being brought into existence, either within us or among us. Therefore, it is a labor that is both purposeful and hopeful.

It is a labor that is, to borrow a phrase from a popular Christmas song, *a labor of love*.

Closing Prayer: O Lord our God, may something new be born in us this day, as well as this season. This season when we celebrate your birth into this cold and cruel world. This season when we rejoice over your amazing arrival to live among us, to give us light and life and hope and peace. We pray this in the name of your Son Jesus. Amen.

Fourth Sunday in Advent

Opening Prayer: Lord God, during this season of Advent, help me to forget and leave behind my old habits, patterns, and ways of thinking and being, so that you might begin a new work in and through me. Help me not to dwell on the *former things*, but to be open and attentive to the *new thing* you have already begun. Amen.

Scripture Reading: Isaiah 43:16-21

This is what the Lord says —
*   he who made a way through the sea,*
*   a path through the mighty waters,*
who drew out the chariots and horses,
*   the army and reinforcements together,*
and they lay there, never to rise again,
*   extinguished, snuffed out like a wick:*
"Forget the former things;
*   do not dwell on the past.*
See, I am doing a new thing!
*   Now it springs up; do you not perceive it?*
I am making a way in the wilderness
*   and streams in the wasteland.*
The wild animals honor me,
*   the jackals and the owls,*
because I provide water in the wilderness
*   and streams in the wasteland,*
to give drink to my people, my chosen,
*   the people I formed for myself*
*   that they may proclaim my praise. (NIV)*

Journal: In what ways do you need to forget the *former things* in order that God can do *a new thing* in or through you?

Reading for Reflection:

Most often in the scriptures it seems like we are called upon to remember, and rightly so. We are called upon to remember how God has moved and how he has worked on our behalf. We are called upon to remember how he has provided for our needs and how he has guided our paths over the course of our lifetime, as well as those of our ancestors. We are called upon to remember how he has protected us from our enemies, defended us from peril, and fought for us when we were too weak, or too powerless, or too exhausted to fight for ourselves. Thus, remembering is a very good thing.

But, interestingly enough, in this instance we are actually called upon to forget. Forgetting, it seems, is also a significant part of the spiritual journey. Especially when we are being called upon to *forget* one thing, in order that God can begin to do a *new* thing. Because somehow not forgetting the *former things* actually keeps us from being able to perceive the *new thing* that is being born within us or among us. But how are we to know when we are to do one as opposed to the other? What does it mean to *forget the former things*? And what *things* are we really talking about here?

Maybe what God is really trying to *get at* in this passage is the idea that at times we have the tendency to hold onto the old at the expense of the new. And when I say old, I am not just referring to the old in a negative sense, I am also referring to old in a more positive way. We seem to have the tendency to think that just because God acted in a particular way, at a particular time and place, that he will always act in just that way. We tend to expect and demand — and even try to determine — how and where and when God will show up in our current story. The problem with that is it keeps us from being open to the *new thing* God seems to be birthing within and among us. If we hold too tightly to the way things "have always been," or to the ways that God has always come thus far, we shut ourselves off to the *new thing* that he is trying to do.

Therefore, we must *forget*. But *forgetting the former things* does not mean forgetting *what* God has done, maybe it only means forgetting *how* he has done them. We should not come to expect, or demand, that he always do things in that particular way from here on out. In that sense *don't dwell on the past* might actually mean *don't live in the past*. Do not limit your vision for, or your openness to, what God might be up to and how he might choose to accomplish it. Don't always expect that he will show up exactly the same way as he did before, or in exactly the same form. If you do that, you will likely miss the *new* that he is trying to bring about.

The season of Advent is that time where we are encouraged to always be ready for however and wherever and whenever God might choose to come. Because he *will* come. A friend of mine reminded me once that, "We come into Advent this year different than we did the last. We are different people, in a different place, with a different set of circumstances." A lot of water has passed under our bridge since we last came to the season of watching and waiting. So, if we are different people, wouldn't it make sense that God would want to come to us in a new and different way? In a way that addresses the time and the place and the season in which we now find ourselves?

Thus, we cannot stubbornly cling to our old ways and demands and expectations, but must be open to receiving this *new thing* that we, thus far, have not perceived. In some way, we must become a blank page, waiting to be filled. The problem with becoming a blank page is that it leaves us both vulnerable and uncomfortable, which, in turn, produces the tendency to try and fill our pages at any and every opportunity.

Therefore, during this season, it might actually take some *emptying* before we are able to perceive, and then receive, this new thing. That's where the *forgetting* comes in. It could be that the story of the nativity has grown so familiar to us that we have forgotten that one of the essential elements of the story in the first place is that God came in a way and a form and a place that no one expected. Should we expect that this Advent and Christmas will be any different?

Closing Prayer: Lord God, help me to be completely open to whatever you are doing in my life and ministry. Help me to be a blank page before you, a lump of clay in the hands of the Master Potter. For your glory. Amen.

Monday
Fourth Week in Advent

If Christmas Eve, skip ahead to December 24

Opening Prayer: O Jesus, you who were born in such small and humble circumstances, help me to always seek the same. You alone know how self-consumed I am and how much I need to grow smaller inside. Yet even those very words sound like a contradiction — *to grow smaller* — but that is truly what I need. It runs against the grain of my selfish heart and, at the same time, strikes a chord deep within me with its goodness and rightness. It brings up a *yes* from the core of my soul, that place where you dwell. It is a call from you, an invitation to grow smaller and smaller and smaller until I disappear completely and there is only you. Give me the courage to follow you on this descending path. In your name and for your sake I pray. Amen.

Scripture Reading: Micah 5:2-5

"But you, Bethlehem Ephrathah,
  though you are small among the clans of Judah,
out of you will come for me
  one who will be ruler over Israel,
whose origins are from of old,
  from ancient times."
Therefore Israel will be abandoned
  until the time when she who is in labor bears a son,
and the rest of his brothers return
  to join the Israelites.

He will stand and shepherd his flock
in the strength of the Lord,
in the majesty of the name of the Lord his God.
And they will live securely, for then his greatness
will reach to the ends of the earth.
And he will be our peace
when the Assyrians invade our land
and march through our fortresses. (NIV)

Journal: Where have you noticed God in a seemingly *small thing* lately?

How did that *small thing* speak to you about him?

How did he come to you through it?

How might God be trying to get your attention in the small details of life this day?

Reading for Reflection:

For quite some time I have been living with the suspicion that God has a preference for the small, the hidden, the quiet, and the lowly. I see it clearly all over the pages of Scripture, but maybe nowhere more clearly than in the Christmas narrative. To imagine that God, the Creator of all that is, chose to enter into that creation in the way that he did is simply astounding. To come into this world as a tiny, helpless baby; born to a couple of poor teenagers who could afford nothing more than a lowly stable for a room, is beyond my imagination. It is almost as if God wanted to slip into our world without being noticed at all, except by those that were watching and waiting — by those paying extra careful attention. Even to the point of being born in tiny Bethlehem.

So, during this season of Advent, would it not be wise for us to try and take notice of the small, the hidden, the quiet, and the ordinary? Would it not be wise to ask ourselves, "If God chose to become smaller in some amazingly mysterious way that we cannot fully comprehend, then how might he be asking us to become smaller as well?" And who knows, if we keep asking ourselves that very question, and if we are really fortunate, then maybe, just maybe, by the end of the week we might actually have become small enough for Christ to arrive, both among us and within us.

Closing Prayer: O Lord, during this day and during this season, help us to be attentive to the small things of this life, knowing full well that great things can come out of them. In the name of Jesus we pray. Amen.

Tuesday
Fourth Week in Advent
If Christmas Eve, skip ahead to December 24

Opening Prayer: Thank you, O God, that you are ever and always *God with us.* Thank you for the gift of this season where we contemplate and celebrate that marvelous truth. Amen.

Scripture Reading: Isaiah 7:10-17

Again the Lord spoke to Ahaz, "Ask the Lord your God for a sign, whether in the deepest depths or in the highest heights."
But Ahaz said, "I will not ask; I will not put the Lord to the test."
Then Isaiah said, "Hear now, you house of David! Is it not enough to try the patience of humans? Will you try the patience of my God also? Therefore the Lord himself will give you a sign: The virgin will conceive and give birth to a son, and will call him Immanuel. He will be eating curds and honey when he knows enough to reject the wrong and choose the right, for before the boy knows enough to reject the wrong and choose the right, the land of the two kings you dread will be laid waste. The Lord will bring on you and on your people and on the house of your father a time unlike any since Ephraim broke away from Judah – he will bring the king of Assyria." (NIV)

Journal: How do you need or want God to be *with you* during this season?

How have you sensed him being *with you* over these last few weeks?

Can you trust that he *is with you* whether you can sense it or not?

Reading for Reflection:

What a promise! And more than just a promise, what a statement of who God is! He is Immanuel! That is his name! Thus, he is the God who just can't stay away. He is God *with us*! In the midst of our deepest darkness, he is *with us*. In the midst of our most desperate loneliness, he is *with us*. In the midst of our most unimaginable pain, he is *with us*. When our hearts have been broken beyond repair, he is *with us*. When we have made a total mess of our lives, he is *with us*. When tragedy strikes, he is *with us*. When we are lost, left, or abandoned, he is *with us*. At the times we feel most unlovable and ashamed, he is *with us*. When we feel like complete and utter failures, he is *with us*. When we feel like all hope is lost, he is *with us*. When we feel completely broken and inept, he is *with us*. When we are terrified of what lies before us, he is *with us*. When we are uncertain about our futures, he is *with us*. And even when life seems to be going *"just fine thank you"* he is *with us* even then. In fact, the psalmist (Psalm 139:7-12) tells us that there is nowhere we can go where he is not with us. Just open your eyes and your ears, he is there. Somewhere. Even if he is there in a way — or a place, or a form — that you didn't expect. He is *with us*! It's just who he is. Thanks be to God.

Closing Prayer: Lord Jesus. Help us to believe that it's true. Help us to truly believe that you are Immanuel — God with us. Help us to believe it in spite of our fears and our uncertainties. Help us to believe it in spite of our anxieties and insecurities. Help us to believe in spite of our loneliness and isolation. And help us to believe in spite of our feelings and our circumstances. Thank you that you are Immanuel, it's just who you are. And since you are Immanuel, which means you will always be with us, help us to seek always to be with you in return. Amen.

Wednesday
Fourth Week in Advent
If Christmas Eve, skip ahead to December 24

Opening Prayer: More of you, Lord Jesus, and less of me, that is my heart's cry. For your glory. Amen.

Scripture Reading: John 3:22-30

After this, Jesus and his disciples went out into the Judean countryside, where he spent some time with them, and baptized. Now John also was baptizing at Aenon near Salim, because there was plenty of water, and people were coming and being baptized. (This was before John was put in prison.) An argument developed between some of John's disciples and a certain Jew over the matter of ceremonial washing. They came to John and said to him, "Rabbi, that man who was with you on the other side of the Jordan — the one you testified about — look, he is baptizing, and everyone is going to him."

To this John replied, "A person can receive only what is given them from heaven. You yourselves can testify that I said, 'I am not the Messiah but am sent ahead of him.' The bride belongs to the bridegroom. The friend who attends the bridegroom waits and listens for him, and is full of joy when he hears the bridegroom's voice. That joy is mine, and it is now complete. He must become greater; I must become less." (NIV)

Journal: How do these words or images speak to your heart and life this day?

What do they inspire within you?

What do they disturb or disrupt within you?

What would it look like in your life to *become less*?

Reading for Reflection:

I don't know about you, but whenever I read these verses about decreasing rather than increasing I immediately start to squirm. They are just so contrary to my nature, so counter-intuitive. I mean, who really wants to decrease, right? And I can never read them without the question arising from God's Spirit deep within me, "So, how's that process going for you these days?"

And, of course, in an effort to avoid the question I immediately start reading the verses around it, trying to see if there is any way of weaseling out of the question through the context. But nope, no luck. No wiggle room. In fact, the context just makes the question more pointed and difficult to answer. The context is that John's disciples had come to him because many of the folks that had come out to the desert to see John had jumped ship and were now going to Jesus instead. "Everyone's going to him," they complained. And John's answer was priceless. *"Good! Let them. Didn't I tell you that I wasn't The One, but only the one sent to bear witness to the One? The bride belongs to the bridegroom, not to me. I'm just a friend of the bridegroom. My job is to attend to the groom; waiting for his arrival, listening for his voice. And when he comes, my job is just to step out of his way. The bride is for him, not for me."*

That's when it hit me. I don't want to be just the friend of the bridegroom, I want to be more than that. I want the attention and affection and recognition that the groom gets. I want the bride to feel that way about me. I want to matter. I don't want to be an insignificant secondary character in this story, I want a bigger role. I want to be the main attraction, or at least *a* main attraction. I want to increase. I want to be BIG in people's lives. I *need* to be BIG in people's lives. And there it was, the whole ugly truth.

So I guess my answer to the original question has to be, "Not very well, I suppose." There is still plenty that needs to die in me, starting with my needy attitude. There is still plenty of *decreasing* that needs to be done, and not just for decreasing's sake, but for his sake — so that he might *increase*. I need to decrease, so that he might be BIG in the lives of people, so that he might grow so BIG that he is all they see, all they want. After all, he is the Beloved Groom, the one who loves them so deeply and passionately that he was willing to sacrifice everything just so they might spend eternity with him.

I pray that I will want nothing more than to help make that happen. I pray that I will learn to step aside and make BIG room for him. I pray that I will not try to take up all the space myself. I pray that I will learn to be a better *friend* of the Bridegroom, rather than being so full of myself. I pray that I might embrace this wonderful life of decreasing. And I pray that the next time he asks me this question, I'll have a better answer.

Closing Prayer:
O Jesus! meek and humble of heart, *Hear me.* From the desire of being esteemed, *Deliver me, Jesus.* From the desire of being loved, *Deliver me, Jesus.* From the desire of being extolled, *Deliver me, Jesus.* From the desire of being honored, *Deliver me, Jesus.* From the desire of being praised, *Deliver me, Jesus.* From the desire of being preferred to others, *Deliver me, Jesus.* From the desire of

being consulted, *Deliver me, Jesus.* From the desire of being approved, *Deliver me, Jesus.*

From the fear of being humiliated, *Deliver me, Jesus.* From the fear of being despised, *Deliver me, Jesus.* From the fear of suffering rebukes, *Deliver me, Jesus.* From the fear of being calumniated, *Deliver me, Jesus.* From the fear of being forgotten, *Deliver me, Jesus.* From the fear of being ridiculed, *Deliver me, Jesus.* From the fear of being wronged, *Deliver me, Jesus.* From the fear of being suspected, *Deliver me, Jesus.*

That others may be loved more than I, *Jesus, grant me the grace to desire it.* That others may be esteemed more than I, *Jesus, grant me the grace to desire it.* That, in the opinion of the world, others may increase and I may decrease, *Jesus, grant me the grace to desire it.* That others may be chosen and I set aside, *Jesus, grant me the grace to desire it.* That others may be praised and I unnoticed, *Jesus, grant me the grace to desire it.* That others may be preferred to me in everything, *Jesus, grant me the grace to desire it.* That others may become holier than I, provided that I may become as holy as I should, *Jesus, grant me the grace to desire it.*

~Litany of Humility

Thursday
Fourth Week in Advent
If Christmas Eve, skip ahead to December 24

Opening Prayer: Lord, awaken me, you whose love burns beyond the stars; light the flame of my lantern that I may always burn with love. ~ Father John Eagan

Scripture Reading: Revelation 3:1-3

"To the angel of the church in Sardis write:
These are the words of him who holds the seven spirits of God and the seven stars. I know your deeds; you have a reputation of being alive, but you are dead. Wake up! Strengthen what remains and is about to die, for I have found your deeds unfinished in the sight of my God. Remember, therefore, what you have received and heard; hold it fast, and repent. But if you do not wake up, I will come like a thief, and you will not know at what time I will come to you." (NIV)

Journal: How do you need to "wake up" these days?

What is about to die in you that needs to be revived?

How are you like the church at Sardis?

How do the words to the church at Sardis speak to your heart today?

Reading for Reflection:

A reputation is a powerful thing. Because a reputation (good or bad) is often not reality, but only someone's impression of reality. And in our day and age—as well as that of the church at Sardis apparently—impression is everything. If you can create and maintain the impression you are hoping for, then who cares what the reality is, right? Thus, impression becomes all about reputation management. What people think about you becomes more important to you than what the truth about you really is. As long as you can keep up the charade it's all good.

But keeping up the charade can be exhausting, and darn near impossible over time. Eventually someone is going to find out the ugly truth. There is always that one person in any crowd that is adept at spotting a phony. Someone who is somehow magically or supernaturally able to see right through the façade—right down to the core. And when this happens we are horrified. Because somehow our greatest fear—and maybe in a strange way our deepest longing as well—comes true, we are exposed.

That's how the church at Sardis must've felt. They had worked and worked at maintaining a good reputation, even though they knew deep in their hearts that there was no life in their souls. And then along comes Jesus, entering into the midst of the pretense, calling their bluff, and tearing their finely crafted costumes to smithereens. At that point they must have been in scramble mode. What do you do? Deny it? Ignore it? Avoid it? Rationalize? Or do you resort to attack? What is the best strategy for damage control? How can we spin it so that our reputation—which we have worked so hard on—still comes out intact?

Or maybe there is another solution. Maybe we do exactly what Jesus is suggesting. Maybe we admit the truth. Maybe we come clean and stop trying to fool ourselves—and others. Maybe we take it as a wake-up call to start living an authentic life with God. Maybe we repent. Maybe we change our minds, our way of thinking, as well as our way of living, and begin to see everything—and live everything—differently. Maybe we realize that reality is more important than reputation and we start trying to be authentic people in Christ, more concerned with how we're loving than with what people are thinking. Like Jesus, who *"made himself of no reputation, and took upon him the form of a servant, and was made in the likeness of men: and being found in fashion as a man, humbled himself, and became obedient unto death, even the death of the cross."* (Philippians 2:7-8, KJV)

Closing Prayer: Most Holy God, awaken me from my soul's deep slumber and bring my life under your complete control. By your grace, awaken me daily to the reality of your presence within and around me. And, by the power of your Spirit, make me responsive to your will and your direction. Amen.

Friday
Fourth Week in Advent
If Christmas Eve, skip ahead to December 24

Opening Prayer: O Lord, my God, protect me from ever having a tepid form of devotion to you. Guard me from having a lukewarm heart. Keep me from ever putting my spiritual life on cruise-control. By your Spirit create a burning desire for you deep within my soul, one that controls and determines the way I live my life. In the name of Jesus I pray. Amen.

Scripture Reading: Revelation 3:14-22

"To the angel of the church in Laodicea write:
These are the words of the Amen, the faithful and true witness, the ruler of God's creation. I know your deeds, that you are neither cold nor hot. I wish you were either one or the other! So, because you are lukewarm – neither hot nor cold – I am about to spit you out of my mouth. You say, 'I am rich; I have acquired wealth and do not need a thing.' But you do not realize that you are wretched, pitiful, poor, blind and naked. I counsel you to buy from me gold refined in the fire, so you can become rich; and white clothes to wear, so you can cover your shameful nakedness; and salve to put on your eyes, so you can see.
Those whom I love I rebuke and discipline. So be earnest and repent. Here I am! I stand at the door and knock. If anyone hears my voice and opens the door, I will come in and eat with that person, and they with me.
To the one who is victorious, I will give the right to sit with me on my throne, just as I was victorious and sat down with my

Father on his throne. Whoever has ears, let them hear what the Spirit says to the churches." (NIV)

Journal: If God were going to write a letter to you today about the state of your heart, what would it say?

What is your spiritual temperature right now?

What is the state of your inner fire?

How are you like the church at Laodicea?

What parts of this letter speak to your heart?

What is God's invitation to you during this season?

Reading for Reflection:
The church at Laodicea was tepid. Wealth and prosperity had lulled them to sleep spiritually. Or, to use the term John uses here, they had become lukewarm. And lukewarm-ness is a trait that God doesn't care for at all. Come to think of it, nobody cares for it. Because being lukewarm reeks of apathy. It has no backbone to it, no commitment, no passion, and no zeal. Which is one of the things God asks the church at Laodicea to become — *zealous.* The word zealous in the Greek is *zēloō,* which means "to boil." God longs for their hearts to boil with love for him. In other words, God is telling them to *turn up the heat* of their affection for him and to be lukewarm no longer.

The image of a stove comes to mind immediately. God is saying, "Right now your passion and desire for me is about a four or five (out of ten). Is that good enough for you? Because it is not good enough for me. I didn't create you to be just a four or five — *turn up the heat.* I want more for you and I want more from you, don't settle for less." I think that's why I love this passage. It is an invitation. God is inviting us into a deeper, more intimate, more passionate relationship with him. God wants our inner lives to boil with affection and desire for him.

The reality is that we all boil inside for something. There is something in our lives that is getting our passion, that is on our front burner. It might be work, it might be family, it might be a significant relationship, it might be wealth (like it was for the Laodiceans), or it might even be ministry. Something is on the front burner of our lives, receiving the heat of our passions and desires, a place that only God deserves. Our challenge is to take the time and the space to figure out what the object of our affections really is, to name it, and to repent—to return God to his rightful place on the front burner of our lives.

One of the ways we do that is given right in the text— by simply opening the door to him, the One who *stands at the door and knocks*. We must consistently open the door of our hearts and invite him into our lives—and our days—to spend intimate time around table of our souls, feasting on the Bread of Life. He will not intrude. He will wait until space has been made and the door has been opened and he has been welcomed in. May we all hear the knock and open the door each day to make space and time for him.

Closing Prayer: Lord Jesus, during this season of Advent, one that usually has us focusing on waiting for you, help us to know that you are also waiting for us. Waiting for us to turn toward you. Waiting for us to hear your knock and hear your voice. Waiting for us to open the door of our hearts and enjoy living union with you. Lord Jesus, give us the strength and the grace to do just that. Turn up the heat of our inner fires of love, Lord Jesus, and let our lives boil with affection and desire. Let our hearts yearn for you and you alone. Amen.

Saturday
Fourth Week in Advent
If Christmas Eve, skip ahead to December 24

Opening Prayer: My God, let me know and love you, so that I may find my happiness in you. Since I cannot fully achieve this on earth, help me to improve daily until I may do so to the full. Enable me to know you ever more on earth, so that I may know you perfectly in heaven. Enable me to love you ever more on earth, so that I may love you perfectly in heaven. In that way my joy may be great on earth, and perfect with you in heaven. O God of truth, grant me the happiness of heaven so that my joy may be full in accord with your promise. In the meantime let my mind dwell on that happiness, my tongue speak of it, my heart pine for it, my mouth pronounce it, my soul hunger for it, my flesh thirst for it, and my entire being desire it until I enter through death in the joy of my Lord forever. Amen. ~St. Augustine

Scripture Reading: Revelation 2:12-17

To the angel of the church in Pergamum write:
  These are the words of him who has the sharp, double-edged sword. I know where you live – where Satan has his throne. Yet you remain true to my name. You did not renounce your faith in me, not even in the days of Antipas, my faithful witness, who was put to death in your city – where Satan lives.
  Nevertheless, I have a few things against you: There are some among you who hold to the teaching of Balaam, who taught Balak to entice the Israelites to sin so that they ate food sacrificed

to idols and committed sexual immorality. Likewise, you also have those who hold to the teaching of the Nicolaitans. Repent therefore! Otherwise, I will soon come to you and will fight against them with the sword of my mouth.

Whoever has ears, let them hear what the Spirit says to the churches. To the one who is victorious, I will give some of the hidden manna. I will also give that person a white stone with a new name written on it, known only to the one who receives it. (NIV)

Journal: What name do you think will be written on your white stone?

What name do you long to be on it?

How does it make you feel that God has a name picked out especially for you?

Reading for Reflection:

One of the constant struggles in the life of faith is to pay attention to the right voices and ignore the wrong ones. That would be especially true if you lived in a place like Pergamum. It was the heart of Enemy territory. The capital city of Evil. It was a place of indulgence, immorality, and deception. It was a place where the wrong voices abounded. And one of the chief strategies of the Enemy is to try and make us believe things about ourselves and about our God that simply aren't true.

In an environment such as this it is vital to hold fast to the truth, lest we get sucked into one of these deceptive ways of thinking. For the truth is our greatest defense against the deceptions of the Enemy. In fact, John tells us in one of his earlier writings that when we come to *know the truth, the truth will set us free* (John 8:32). Maybe that's why Jesus uses the image of a sword (his word) as the means by which he will wage war against the Enemy. His truth is our main offensive weapon. It is the thing we can use to destroy the lies of the Deceiver and hold fast to the truth of our Creator. When we hold fast to the truth about our God and about ourselves we will be free men and women.

The truth is, our God is so filled with love for us that he has a special name picked out for each one of us—a pet name, if you will. It is a name of deep affection that will bear our true identity. One that will immediately let us know how incredibly valuable we are to him and how extravagantly loved we are by him. It is a name written on a white stone that he will share with us when we are united with him in the heavenly realms for all of eternity.

It is a name that is the truest expression of who we really are. It is a name that is just too good to be true, yet it is both too good and too true. And I am convinced that when we hear it, a deep "yes" will rise up from the core of our being. I can't wait.

Closing Prayer: O Lord, my God, thank you that you have a name picked out especially for me, one that has been hand-picked by you with me specifically and uniquely in mind. When I am tempted to believe the lies of the Deceiver about who you are and who I am to you, give me a little hint about what my true name really is, so that I may know the truth that will set me free. The truth that you love me more than I could hope for in my wildest dreams. As I watch and wait for your return, help me to hold fast to this truth in my heart and mind. In Christ. Amen.

December 24 – Christmas Eve

Opening Prayer: O Lord, the time has almost come. Just a few more hours and we will once again celebrate your *coming* into this dark and broken world. Soon the light will dawn, our hearts will be enlarged, and our joy will be increased. We wait, O Lord, in silence and wonder and hope for your arrival among us and within us. Come, Lord Jesus. Amen.

Scripture Reading: Isaiah 9:1-7

Nevertheless, there will be no more gloom for those who were in distress. In the past he humbled the land of Zebulun and the land of Naphtali, but in the future he will honor Galilee of the nations, by the Way of the Sea, beyond the Jordan –
The people walking in darkness
*   have seen a great light;*
on those living in the land of deep darkness
*   a light has dawned.*
You have enlarged the nation
*   and increased their joy;*
they rejoice before you
*   as people rejoice at the harvest,*
as warriors rejoice
*   when dividing the plunder.*
For as in the day of Midian's defeat,
*   you have shattered*
the yoke that burdens them,
*   the bar across their shoulders,*
*   the rod of their oppressor.*
Every warrior's boot used in battle

and every garment rolled in blood
will be destined for burning,
  will be fuel for the fire.
For to us a child is born,
  to us a son is given,
  and the government will be on his shoulders.
And he will be called
  Wonderful Counselor, Mighty God,
  Everlasting Father, Prince of Peace.
Of the greatness of his government and peace
  there will be no end.
He will reign on David's throne
  and over his kingdom,
establishing and upholding it
  with justice and righteousness
  from that time on and forever.
The zeal of the Lord Almighty
  will accomplish this. (NIV)

Journal: Which name of Jesus seems most significant to your heart and life these days? Why?

Reading for Reflection:

If ever a night is filled with wonder and anticipation, it is this one. For children it is simply magical; all of the packages wrapped and waiting under the tree, just begging to be torn into when morning finally arrives. We count down the days—and even the hours and minutes—filled with longing, which eventually gives way to joyful expectancy. Finally, the time has come. Finally the waiting is over and the celebration can begin. It seems like we've been waiting forever.

Israel had waited hundreds of years. They had waited through captivity and oppression and affliction—even through a lengthy silence from their God. And now, unbeknownst to them, the time was at hand. The hope-filled words that Isaiah had uttered some 700 years earlier were about to come true. The greatest gift of all time—what Paul would later call *God's indescribable gift* (2 Corinthians 9:15)—was about to be born into the world. And this gift—Jesus—would be more than anyone ever dreamt about in their wildest dreams. In fact, this gift would be called Wonderful. Counselor. Mighty God. Everlasting Father. Prince of Peace. The One full of wonder and wisdom and strength and love. The One able to bring about wholeness in the midst of this chaotic and broken world. It seems too good to be true.

What happens within you as wait for his impending arrival? What happens within you as you hear these names? What kind of God have you been waiting for and hoping for and longing for? How do you long for him to show up in the midst of your life and world? How do you need for him to show up in the midst of your life and world? Which of the names uttered by the prophet Isaiah makes something dead or dying come to life in you? Thank goodness Christmas is finally here.

Closing Prayer: Make room in our hearts, Lord Jesus, as we prepare to receive you. For unto us, this very night, a Child is born. Unto us a Savior is given. Thanks be to God. Amen.

December 25 – Christmas Day

Opening Prayer: Lord Jesus, today we celebrate your birth. Today we rejoice in the fact that our Almighty God has come down to make his dwelling among us. Help us to join our voices with the heavenly chorus that bursts into song this day singing: "Glory to God in the highest, and on earth peace to those upon whom his favor rests." May our hearts rejoice in you, Lord Jesus. Amen.

Scripture Reading: Luke 2:1-14

In those days Caesar Augustus issued a decree that a census should be taken of the entire Roman world. (This was the first census that took place while Quirinius was governor of Syria.) And everyone went to their own town to register.

So Joseph also went up from the town of Nazareth in Galilee to Judea, to Bethlehem the town of David, because he belonged to the house and line of David. He went there to register with Mary, who was pledged to be married to him and was expecting a child. While they were there, the time came for the baby to be born, and she gave birth to her firstborn, a son. She wrapped him in cloths and placed him in a manger, because there was no guest room available for them.

And there were shepherds living out in the fields nearby, keeping watch over their flocks at night. An angel of the Lord appeared to them, and the glory of the Lord shone around them, and they were terrified. But the angel said to them, "Do not be afraid. I bring you good news that will cause great joy for all the people. Today in the town of David a Savior has been born to you; he is the Messiah, the Lord. This will be a sign to you: You will find a baby wrapped in cloths and lying in a manger."

Suddenly a great company of the heavenly host appeared with the angel, praising God and saying, "Glory to God in the highest heaven, and on earth peace to those on whom his favor rests." (NIV)

Journal: What is going on in your heart and soul today as you celebrate the birth of Jesus?

What words of the Christmas narrative bring something new alive in you today?

How will you make room for him today?

Reading for Reflection:

She wrapped him in cloths and placed him in a manger, because there was no room for them in the inn. (Luke 2:6-7)

Room is a very important thing in the life of the Spirit. As a matter of fact, any kind of new birth seems to require it. Ironically, and unfortunately, during this season, just as in the time of Mary and Joseph, it is so easy for life just to fill up. Even on this day! Particularly on this day. And when life is over-filled there is simply no room for any new thing of the Spirit to be born in us; the pace and demands of the season are at odds with the room and reflection necessary to pay attention to how, where, and when God might be entering our lives and our world.

Maybe that's why the words of the old Christmas carol—which we sing on this very morning—remind us to, "Let every heart prepare him room." It seems that the writers of those wonderful songs of old knew well the secret that unless we work diligently to make room for him, it will not simply happen on its own. In the words of Richard Foster, it will not just "fall on our heads." Making room takes effort and intention and prayer and planning. And unless we are willing and able to put forth the energy and effort to pay attention, it is likely that when he does eventually come, we will be like the rest of the world on that sleepy Christmas morning and miss him too.

Closing Prayer: Lord God, in this holy season of song, prayer, and laughter, may we praise you for the amazing wonders you have sent us. For shining stars, angel's songs, and the newborn's cry in a lowly manger, we thank you. We praise you for the Word made flesh. May we behold his glory and bask in his radiance. Be with us as we celebrate this Christmas season. Amen.

December 26
The Second Day of Christmas

Opening Prayer: Lord Jesus, thank you that we get the opportunity to celebrate your birth for an entire season, rather than just one day. During these next days and weeks help us to be attentive to whatever you desire to bring to life within us as a result of your birth into this dark and hurting world. Amen.

Scripture Reading: Luke 2:15-21

When the angels had left them and gone into heaven, the shepherds said to one another, "Let's go to Bethlehem and see this thing that has happened, which the Lord has told us about."

So they hurried off and found Mary and Joseph, and the baby, who was lying in the manger. When they had seen him, they spread the word concerning what had been told them about this child, and all who heard it were amazed at what the shepherds said to them. But Mary treasured up all these things and pondered them in her heart. The shepherds returned, glorifying and praising God for all the things they had heard and seen, which were just as they had been told.

On the eighth day, when it was time to circumcise the child, he was named Jesus, the name the angel had given him before he was conceived. (NIV)

Journal: What things have you treasured or pondered lately?

How have you treasured and pondered Jesus in the last few weeks?

What treasures have you uncovered?

Reading for Reflection:

What makes you the best version of yourself? For me I think it has a lot to do with two words: *treasuring* and *pondering*. When I am taking time to *ponder* what God is doing within and around me, and to *treasure* whatever that may be — or more importantly, to treasure the One who is doing those things — then I tend to be my very best self.

The word used here for *treasure* in the Greek is *syntereo*, which means "to attend to with great care." It gives the impression that you completely realize that you're holding something of immense value in your hands (or in your heart), so you take the very best care of *it* you possibly can. You marvel at *it*, you behold its beauty, you gaze upon *it*, and you are fully captured by *it*. And the word for *ponder* is *symballo,* which means "to bring together in one's mind." It is to think deeply about, to reflect upon, to consider the value and the implications of. The two really go hand-in-hand.

The saints and the poets throughout history have used different words and images to capture these two concepts, as well as to help us understand how to practice them. Julian of Norwich once wrote: "Truth sees God, and wisdom beholds God, and from these two comes the third, and that is a marvelous delight in God, which is love." And A. W. Tozer wrote: "Faith is the gaze of the soul upon a saving God." Mother Teresa once said, "By contemplation the soul draws directly from the heart of God the graces which the active life must distribute." And finally, author Marian Scheele once wrote, "When the soul is occupied by looking away from present trials into the face of Christ, and making this a regular and passionate occupation, this soul will become more tranquil and still, and therefore more able to reflect the Being it adores."

My guess is that how well we are doing at *treasuring* and *pondering* will directly affect the quality and depth of our lives. Therefore the question becomes: "How am I doing at *treasuring* and *pondering* what God is up to within me and around me these days?" Which then begs the question, "What is God up to within me and around me these days?" Unless we make some time and space to consider these questions, and to treasure and ponder the answers, we will never really stand a chance of being the very best version of ourselves—the version that God dreamt us to be.

And that doesn't just carry implications for us, but implications for those God has called us to as well. We must be very good stewards of whatever God is doing in and around us because that very *treasure* is not only what God has given to nurture and feed our souls, but also the *treasure* he has given us to give away to those in our lives and world. I think that's what Jesus was getting at when he said in Matthew: "Therefore every teacher of the law who has been instructed about the kingdom of heaven is like the owner of a house who brings out of his storeroom new *treasures* as well as old." (Matthew 13:52)

So today, let us all *treasure* and *ponder*. Because as we treasure and ponder our great God we will find that we are the ones treasured and pondered by the One who loves us, treasures us, and delights in us more than we dare ask or imagine. Thanks be to God!

Closing Prayer: Jesus, help us to learn the art of treasuring and pondering. May we, like your mother before us, make time and space to consider the beauty and the mystery and the wonder of all this season has to offer. Help us to marvel at who you are and what you are doing in our lives and in our world. Amen.

December 27
The Third Day of Christmas

Opening Prayer: We beseech Thee, O Lord, let our hearts be graciously enlightened by Thy holy radiance, that we may serve Thee without fear in holiness and righteousness all the days of our life; that so we may escape the darkness of this world, and by Thy guidance attain the land of eternal brightness; through Thy mercy, O blessed Lord, Who doest live and govern all things, world without end. Amen. ~Sarum Breviary, 1085 C.E.

Scripture Reading: Luke 2:21-40

On the eighth day, when it was time to circumcise the child, he was named Jesus, the name the angel had given him before he was conceived.

When the time came for the purification rites required by the Law of Moses, Joseph and Mary took him to Jerusalem to present him to the Lord (as it is written in the Law of the Lord, "Every firstborn male is to be consecrated to the Lord"), and to offer a sacrifice in keeping with what is said in the Law of the Lord: "a pair of doves or two young pigeons."

Now there was a man in Jerusalem called Simeon, who was righteous and devout. He was waiting for the consolation of Israel, and the Holy Spirit was on him. It had been revealed to him by the Holy Spirit that he would not die before he had seen the Lord's Messiah. Moved by the Spirit, he went into the temple courts. When the parents brought in the child Jesus to do for him what the custom of the Law required, Simeon took him in his arms and praised God, saying:

"Sovereign Lord, as you have promised,
   you may now dismiss your servant in peace.
For my eyes have seen your salvation,
   which you have prepared in the sight of all nations:
a light for revelation to the Gentiles,
   and the glory of your people Israel."

The child's father and mother marveled at what was said about him. Then Simeon blessed them and said to Mary, his mother: "This child is destined to cause the falling and rising of many in Israel, and to be a sign that will be spoken against, so that the thoughts of many hearts will be revealed. And a sword will pierce your own soul too."

There was also a prophet, Anna, the daughter of Penuel, of the tribe of Asher. She was very old; she had lived with her husband seven years after her marriage, and then was a widow until she was eighty-four. She never left the temple but worshiped night and day, fasting and praying. Coming up to them at that very moment, she gave thanks to God and spoke about the child to all who were looking forward to the redemption of Jerusalem.

When Joseph and Mary had done everything required by the Law of the Lord, they returned to Galilee to their own town of Nazareth. And the child grew and became strong; he was filled with wisdom, and the grace of God was on him. (NIV)

Journal: Where do you find yourself in today's passage?

Who can you most relate to? Why?

What does God have to say to you through them?

How do the words *"And a sword will pierce your soul too"* strike you?

Reading for Reflection:

Surely as Simeon spoke these words to Joseph and Mary, telling them all of the incredible things about their newborn baby, our Savior, they wouldn't have just slipped by unnoticed. Can you imagine how disturbing these words must have been to the new parents? Can you imagine how disturbing they would be now if someone uttered them to you this very day? "What do you mean *a sword will pierce my own soul too*? What is that supposed to mean? What in the world does that even look like? And how will it happen? How incredibly painful that sounds. It would be painful enough for a sword to pierce my body, but piercing my soul sounds even worse, like another whole level of pain and suffering altogether." Just ask those who have experienced it. They know it all too well.

And *too*. What do you mean by *too*? Is my newborn baby's soul going to be pierced by a sword as well? Please, just pierce me and leave this precious little one's soul in one piece. To have the heart and soul of the one I love *pierced* is more than I can bear—way worse than if it merely happened to me. But, then again, nobody knows that more than *the* Father, the One from whom all fatherhood derives its name. If our souls can be pierced by tragedy, or loss, or desolation, imagine his very own soul being *pierced* to the core. Why on earth would God allow his own soul to be *pierced*? Or even more, his own son's? Something beautiful and life-giving must happen in the midst of the piercing: his, Joseph's, Mary's, and even ours. But even that certainly doesn't take away the depths of the pain.

So, as excited as Mary and Joseph must've been with angels and shepherds and stars and wise men and gifts and prophesies and such, somehow this one little line must've stopped them in their tracks. Surely this strange and awful phrase must've lingered in the backs of their minds and disrupted them, at least a little. So as we celebrate the gifts of these twelve days of Christmas, and the incredible Gift given both to us and for us, let us recognize, and embrace—as did Mary and Joseph—the notion that maybe, just maybe, Simeon's terribly disruptive words are somehow meant for us as well.

Closing Prayer: And now, O Lord, finally, allow your servant to depart in peace, as you have promised. For with my very own eyes I have seen your coming into this dark and hurting world. I have seen you show up, bringing your salvation, for which the world has been longing for centuries. You, O Light, have finally come into our darkness in order that we—all people—might see your truth and give glory to you, our great and mighty God! Amen.

December 28
The Fourth Day of Christmas

Opening Prayer: Most High, glorious God, enlighten the darkness of my heart, and give me right faith, certain hope, and perfect charity, wisdom and understanding, Lord, that I may carry out your holy and true command. Amen. ~St. Francis of Assisi

Scripture Reading: Matthew 2:13-23

But after they had gone, the angel of the Lord appeared to Joseph in a dream and said, "Get up now, take the little child and his mother and escape to Egypt. Stay there until I tell you. For Herod means to seek out the child and kill him."

So Joseph got up, and taking the child and his mother with him in the middle of the night, set off for Egypt, where he remained until Herod's death. This again is a fulfilment of the Lord's word spoken through the prophet – 'Out of Egypt I called my son'.

When Herod saw that he had been fooled by the wise men he was furiously angry. He issued orders, and killed all the male children of two years and under in Bethlehem and the surrounding district – basing his calculation on his careful questioning of the wise men.

Then Jeremiah's prophecy was fulfilled: 'A voice was heard in Ramah, lamentation, weeping and great mourning, Rachel weeping for her children, refusing to be comforted, because they were no more'.

But after Herod's death an angel of the Lord again appeared to Joseph in a dream and said, "Now get up and take the infant

and his mother with you and go into the land of Israel. For those who sought the child's life are dead."

So Joseph got up and took the little child and his mother with him and journeyed towards the land of Israel. But when he heard that Archelaus was now reigning as king of Judea in the place of his father Herod, he was afraid to enter the country. Then he received warning in a dream to turn aside into the district of Galilee and came to live in a small town called Nazareth – thus fulfilling the old prophecy, that he should be called a Nazarene. (JBP)

Journal: What do you do with these verses from Matthew's gospel?

Is there a weeping or mourning that you are being asked to endure during this season? What is it?

How are you bearing it?

Where is God in the midst of it?

Reading for Reflection:

Right in the middle of this joyful season of celebrating the extraordinary gift of God's coming into our dark world, we get this stark reminder of just how dark our world and dire our need is for a Savior. Today is referred to as *The Feast of Holy Innocents* on the church calendar. It is the time when we remember the slaughter of innocent children by King Herod in his attempt to kill the infant Jesus. Herod was so threatened by the idea of losing his throne to this newborn King that he would go to any length to make sure his power and his position were not taken away from him. It is a vivid reminder to what lengths we fallen humans will go to preserve and defend our self-centered ways once they are threatened. In fact, we do it all the time, just not so obviously or violently. Ours is a much more subtle, covert operation, usually involving words as weapons.

Closing Prayer: Lord God, what a hard reminder that things are never neat and tidy in this life, but often messy and painful. We cannot escape the pain and brokenness of this life no matter how hard we try. There is no way out, only through. Thank you that you are that way through. In you there is hope that one day all things will be redeemed, even the evil of our own hearts. Lord, have mercy! Amen.

December 29
The Fifth Day of Christmas

Opening Prayer: God be in my head, and in my understanding; God be in my eyes, and in my looking; God be in my mouth, and in my speaking; God be in my heart, and in my thinking; God be at my end, and at my departing. ~Sarum Primer, 16th century

Scripture Reading: Luke 2:41-52

Every year at the Passover festival Jesus' parents used to go to Jerusalem. When he was twelve years old they went up to the city as usual for the festival. When it was over they started back home, but the boy Jesus stayed behind in Jerusalem, without his parents' knowledge. They went a day's journey assuming that he was somewhere in their company, and then they began to look for him among their relations and acquaintances. They failed to find him, however, and turned back to the city, looking for him as they went. Three days later, they found him – in the Temple, sitting among the teachers, listening to them and asking them questions. All those who heard him were astonished at his powers of comprehension and at the answers that he gave. When Joseph and Mary saw him, they could hardly believe their eyes, and his mother said to him, "Why have you treated us like this, my son? Here have your father and I been very worried, looking for you everywhere!"

And Jesus replied, "But why were you looking for me? Did you not know that I must be in my Father's house?"

But they did not understand his reply. Then he went home with them to Nazareth and was obedient to them. And his mother treasured all these things in her heart. And as Jesus

continued to grow in body and mind, he grew also in the love of God and of those who knew him. (JBP)

Journal: Where have you been *looking everywhere* for Jesus this season?

Where did you find him?

Where are the places you can always find him?

Have you looked there?

Reading for Reflection:

There is a lot written in the scriptures about being lost and being found — be it a *lost* son or a *lost* coin or a *lost* sheep. And each instance, it seems, has a little different slant to it, a different emphasis. Sometimes we are the ones cast in the role of being lost and sometimes we are cast in the role of being found. Sometimes we are even the ones doing the finding. It can be a little confusing. I mean, who is the one that is really lost and who is the one that's actually doing the finding? And is it possible that I might think I am the finder when I am actually the findee?

That's what makes this story so interesting. Mary and Joseph think Jesus is lost and launch an all-out search in order to find him again. But once they find him they realize that he was never really lost in the first place. He was actually right where he was supposed to be. *"Why were you looking for me?"* he replied, *"Don't you know me well enough by now? Don't you know that I had to be in my father's house? If you are ever looking for me, this is where you will find me."*

Maybe you and I would do well to remember that. Because sometimes it is easy for us to lose track of Jesus too. Sometimes, no matter how hard we try, we just can't seem to find him, or to connect with him. In those times it is easy for us to feel as if we have somehow lost him, which is impossible. That's when we must remember that there are certain places where he can always be found; be it in his house, or in his word, or even in our hearts — his Spirit living within us. Those are places where he *must* be. Just look there. And if we look long enough and search hard enough eventually we will find him, or he will find us, however that's supposed to work.

Closing Prayer: Thank you, Lord Jesus, that in spite of how it might feel or appear at times, you are never lost. In fact, you are always the one doing the finding, it is just who you are. Thank you that you relentlessly pursue our hearts until they completely belong to you. That is what we celebrate during the Christmas season. Thanks be to God.

December 30
The Sixth Day of Christmas

Opening Prayer: O Christ, visible expression of the invisible God, thank you for leaving the glory of heaven and coming to earth that we might see with our own eyes the face of God and hear with our own ears the voice of God. And that we might truly come to know the heart of God through you. Amen.

Scripture Reading: John 1:1-18

At the beginning God expressed himself. That personal expression, that word, was with God, and was God, and he existed with God from the beginning. All creation took place through him, and none took place without him. In him appeared life and this life was the light of mankind. The light still shines in the darkness and the darkness has never put it out.

A man called John was sent by God as a witness to the light, so that any man who heard his testimony might believe in the light. This man was not himself the light: he was sent simply as a personal witness to that light.

That was the true light which shines upon every man as he comes into the world. He came into the world – the world he had created – and the world failed to recognise him. He came into his own creation, and his own people would not accept him. Yet wherever men did accept him he gave them the power to become sons of God. These were the men who truly believed in him, and their birth depended not on the course of nature nor on any impulse or plan of man, but on God.

So the word of God became a human being and lived among us. We saw his splendour (the splendour as of a father's only son), full of grace and truth. And it was about him that John stood up and testified, exclaiming: "Here is the one I was speaking about when I said that although he would come after me he would always be in front of me; for he existed before I was born!" Indeed, every one of us has shared in his riches – there is a grace in our lives because of his grace. For while the Law was given by Moses, love and truth came through Jesus Christ. It is true that no one has ever seen God at any time. Yet the divine and only Son, who lives in the closest intimacy with the Father, has made him known. (JBP)

Journal: What does the relatedness (intimacy) of the Trinity say to us about God?

What does it say about how and why we were made?

What does it say about what God longs for with us and for us?

What does it say about how we should relate to one another?

Reading for Reflection:

Before the beginning there was a Heart and this Heart was the substance of God. It came from the very core of who God was and was the very essence of God from before the beginning.

Through his Heart God created all things, without it nothing received the life-blood of God. This Heart was the source of true *shalom*. Its blood gave us the ability to see — to see the depths of the Heart in spite of all darkness because the darkness is unable stop its beating.

And God ripped his Heart from his very chest and he transplanted that Heart into one like us, wrapping it in flesh and bones and giving him a face and a name. And God's Heart lived with us. He walked with us, talked with us, laughed and cried with us, and we saw what God's Heart looked like; it was pumping with the blood of grace and truth.

Closing Prayer: O God, Three and One, how you long for us, who are made in your image, to enter into the intimate life of the Trinity. So much so that you came to earth to make a way for that to happen. May we enter into to the joyful union of the Trinity. And may we live in love as we live in you. May we indeed join in the Great Round Dance of Love for all eternity. Amen.

December 31
The Seventh Day of Christmas

Opening Prayer: Give us the courage and the strength, O Jesus, to follow your invitation downward, whatever that might look like. Help us to know that since you emptied yourself and made yourself nothing, we should strive to do the same. Make it our ambition, Lord Jesus, to be like you. Amen.

Scripture Reading: Philippians 2:1-13

Therefore if you have any encouragement from being united with Christ, if any comfort from his love, if any common sharing in the Spirit, if any tenderness and compassion, then make my joy complete by being like-minded, having the same love, being one in spirit and of one mind. Do nothing out of selfish ambition or vain conceit. Rather, in humility value others above yourselves, not looking to your own interests but each of you to the interests of the others.

In your relationships with one another, have the same mindset as Christ Jesus:

Who, being in very nature God,
did not consider equality with God something to be
used to his own advantage;
rather, he made himself nothing
by taking the very nature of a servant,
being made in human likeness.
And being found in appearance as a man,
he humbled himself

by becoming obedient to death —
even death on a cross!
Therefore God exalted him to the highest place
and gave him the name that is above every name,
that at the name of Jesus every knee should bow,
in heaven and on earth and under the earth,
and every tongue acknowledge that Jesus Christ is Lord,
to the glory of God the Father.

Therefore, my dear friends, as you have always obeyed — not only in my presence, but now much more in my absence — continue to work out your salvation with fear and trembling, for it is God who works in you to will and to act in order to fulfill his good purpose. (NIV)

Journal: What does it look like specifically in your life to *have the same mindset as that of Christ Jesus?*

How is God asking you to make yourself nothing?

Reading for Reflection: O Jesus, how far down you had to come to reach us. How small and how low. Can anyone really comprehend the magnitude of that downward journey? You, who had always enjoyed true delight, the loving intimacy of the Trinity, were willing to step out of the ecstasy of that intimacy because of your great desire to bring us into it. You, who were *in very nature God*, laid aside your Divine privilege and position to become *a man of sorrows, despised and rejected by men.* You, the Eternal One, willing to become a mere mortal. You, the Creator of all, willing to become one of the created. O the great sacrifice! O the immense love! You, O Christ, emptied yourself of more than we can ever comprehend or imagine. You, O Christ, made yourself *of no reputation* (Phil. 2:7 KJV). And you, O Christ, have given us an example, that we might do the same. Lord Jesus, during this season when we celebrate your stepping down out of the throne room of heaven to become one of us, show us what this emptying looks like for each of us in the days ahead.

Closing Prayer: O Lord, as we come to the end of another year and as we reflect on all that has been, as well as look ahead to all that will be, help us to know what we need to empty ourselves of in order to *have this mind among ourselves which was also in Christ Jesus.* All for your glory. Amen.

January 1
The Eighth Day of Christmas

Opening Prayer: God, who would you have me to be and what would you have me to do in the New Year that lies ahead? It is so full of promise and so full of possibility, but it is also so easy to go astray. It is easy to be pulled and swayed and distracted by my own needs and agendas, by my own desires for acceptance and attention and affirmation and significance. Help me, O Lord, to be led by your Spirit rather than by all of the contrary voices around and within me. Help me to follow your voice alone in this New Year. Amen.

Scripture Reading: Psalm 131:1-3

O Lord, my heart is not lifted up;
*   my eyes are not raised too high;*
I do not occupy myself with things
*   too great and too marvelous for me.*
But I have calmed and quieted my soul,
*   like a weaned child with its mother;*
*   like a weaned child is my soul within me.*
O Israel, hope in the Lord
*   from this time forth and forevermore. (ESV)*

Journal: What are your deepest prayers and longings for the year ahead?

What do you most deeply long for in your relationship with God?

How will you move in the direction of that desire?

Reading for Reflection:

I think I might adopt Psalm 131 as my prayer for the New Year because it reminds me of what is really important and what God seems to desire as far as my outlook and my attitude are concerned. All of which is the polar opposite of everything the culture and the world encourages me to pursue. In a culture that says, *"Make a name for yourself, achieve, perform, jockey for position, be ambitious, accomplish much!"* this perspective can seem odd, if not the exact opposite.

Can you imagine someone asking about your goals for the New Year, or about your New Year's resolutions, and telling them, "Well, I'm trying to keep my heart from being too high or proud. I'm trying not to get too full of myself. And I'm going to try not to *be lifted up* — in my own eyes, or the eyes of those around me. I'm actually kind of hoping that I become smaller, less significant, and less visible. I want to stay out of the limelight and be about the things that no one ever really sees. I want to make sure that I *don't occupy myself — my heart, mind, and soul — with things that are simply too great and marvelous for me.* I'm actually kind of hoping that my soul will be stilled, *calmed and quieted, like a weaned child with its mother* — totally content just to *be*, totally dependent on God and his great care and affection. I really just want to be held by him and loved by him. I don't want to put my hope in what I do or what I achieve or what I accomplish. I don't want to put my confidence in my own gifts, abilities, and efforts. I want to put my hope totally in the Lord, both now and forevermore." What kind of response do you think that line of thinking would get?

But that is what I long for, and more importantly, what I think God longs for in me—just to be his. Not to be heroic, or epic, or wonderful, or legendary. Not to be popular, or admired, or successful, or productive. But simply to be his and to be loved and to be obedient and just let everything else take care of itself. Happy New Year.

Closing Prayer: God, I'm not trying to rule the roost, I don't want to be king of the mountain. I haven't meddled where I have no business or fantasized grandiose plans. I've kept my feet on the ground, I've cultivated a quiet heart. Like a baby content in its mother's arms, my soul is a baby content. Wait, Israel, for God. Wait with hope. Hope now; hope always! (Psalm 131, *The Message*)

January 2
The Ninth Day of Christmas

Opening Prayer: O Jesus, speak to me during this time about the story you are telling, the story I was made for. Open my eyes, Lord, to the ways that story is being told and lived in the events and circumstances of this day. Show me how all that happens to me this day echoes your larger Story if only I will keep my heart focused on you. In your name I pray. Amen.

Scripture Reading: Luke 1:1-4

Inasmuch as many have undertaken to compile a narrative of the things that have been accomplished among us, just as those who from the beginning were eyewitnesses and ministers of the word have delivered them to us, it seemed good to me also, having followed all things closely for some time past, to write an orderly account for you, most excellent Theophilus, that you may have certainty concerning the things you have been taught. (ESV)

Journal: What *narrative* is being written in you these days?

How does the Christmas narrative speak into your own at this point in your journey?

Reading for Reflection:

I love the way Luke begins his gospel. It reminds me that with God there is always a *narrative* being *compiled*, both within me and around me. It is something that I must pay careful attention to, especially during this season, or else I can easily miss it altogether. What exactly is the story God is writing within me these days? What is he doing deep in my heart and soul? How is he drawing me to deeper and deeper places with himself? How is he trying to disrupt or disturb me in order to make me more fully his own? What is he inviting me to? What is he asking of me? How is he being born anew within and around me? Am I living his story for me in every way possible? Or am I somehow resisting, refusing, ignoring, or denying it?

There are other narratives within me that compete with his—ones that make the story I end up living each day much darker, much uglier, much less heroic. They are *false narratives* that go deep into my soul; planted there long ago by the arrows that have pierced my heart along the way, as well as what I've interpreted those arrows to mean concerning my value, worth, and identity. They are the tools of the enemy to keep me living in a bad, dark, hopeless story, rather than the good, beautiful, heroic one that God so deeply longs for me to live in. As well as the story he so desperately wants to live in me.

So I guess the truth of the matter is that every day I have to choose which story I'm going to be about, in which story I am going to live. Am I going to be like Luke and be about *compiling a narrative* of all that God is doing in and through me? Or am I going to live a story that is much less than the story He has imagined for and with me? Doesn't sound like much of a choice, does it?

Closing Prayer: Father, compile your narrative in and through me today. Write your story upon my heart and life, that I may be an open book about you, so that others might read of your unending love on every page. In the name of Jesus, the author of our faith. Amen.

January 3
The Tenth Day of Christmas

Opening Prayer: Jesus, thank you that you are so much bigger than the little boxes we try to put you in. Thank you that you are so much more than our minds can conceive, or even imagine. Thank you that we can never get to the end of you, there is always more to know, always more to love. Expand our picture of you today, and every day, Lord Jesus. Amen.

Scripture Reading: Colossians 1:15-23, 2:9-10

Christ is the visible image of the invisible God.
He existed before anything was created and is supreme over all creation,
for through him God created everything
in the heavenly realms and on earth.
He made the things we can see
and the things we can't see —
such as thrones, kingdoms, rulers, and authorities in the unseen world.
Everything was created through him and for him.
He existed before anything else,
and he holds all creation together.
Christ is also the head of the church,
which is his body.
He is the beginning,
supreme over all who rise from the dead.
So he is first in everything.
For God in all his fullness

was pleased to live in Christ,
and through him God reconciled
everything to himself.
He made peace with everything in heaven and on earth
by means of Christ's blood on the cross. (NLT)

Yet it is in him that God gives a full and complete expression of himself. Moreover, your own completeness is only realised in him, who is the authority over all authorities, and the supreme power over all powers. (JBP)

Journal: Who is Jesus to you?

Who do the scriptures say that he is?

Make a list of characteristics that you think describe him. Now do the same for God the Father. Look at your lists. What catches your attention?

Reading for Reflection:

A. W. Tozer once said that *what comes into our minds when we think about God is probably the most important thing about us.* That is probably because the picture we have of God—what we really believe to be true about him—has such a significant impact on the way we live our lives. As a matter of fact, if you want to know what you really believe about God, just take a look at how you're living your life and it will give you a pretty good indication.

For example, if you are like me and struggle with anxiety and control issues, it might mean that you have a hard time believing God really cares for you—that he can be fully trusted with every detail of your life. Or if you struggle with insecurity and a lack of self-worth, it could mean that you have a hard time believing that God could really love someone like you. Or if you are constantly battling busyness and performance issues, it may mean that you believe that God's love and favor has to be earned. Unfortunately, the possibilities are endless. But one thing is for sure, looking at your life can be a telling proposition.

I guess God knew this. I guess he knew how difficult and confusing life and faith can be at times. I guess he knew that we would have all kinds of wrong ideas and misconceptions about who he really is. I guess that's why he just could not stay away. I guess that's why he left the throne room of heaven and came down to earth. I guess that's why he showed us his face, so we would know beyond a shadow of a doubt what he really looks like. I guess that's why he sent Jesus, the *visible expression of the invisible God.* He didn't want us guessing. He didn't want us to be in the dark. He had a deep desire for us to know the truth about his heart and his character, so that if we ever start to wonder what he is really like, we can just look at Jesus and know for sure. Because, ultimately God is Christ-like. Jesus is the best picture God ever had taken of himself.

Closing Prayer: Lord Jesus, thanks that in you the whole fullness of deity dwells in bodily form. Not just in part, not just a piece, but in full. You are fully God and yet fully man. O the mystery! The invisible, intangible God has made himself visible and tangible in you. Thank you for being willing to do that. Amen.

January 4
The Eleventh Day of Christmas

Opening Prayer: O Lord, our God, thank you for the incredible gift of Jesus, the final and ultimate word about who you are and how you feel about us. Amen.

Scripture Reading: Hebrews 1:1-4

In the past God spoke to our ancestors through the prophets at many times and in various ways, but in these last days he has spoken to us by his Son, whom he appointed heir of all things, and through whom also he made the universe. The Son is the radiance of God's glory and the exact representation of his being, sustaining all things by his powerful word. After he had provided purification for sins, he sat down at the right hand of the Majesty in heaven. So he became as much superior to the angels as the name he has inherited is superior to theirs. (NIV)

Journal: How has God spoken to you recently?

What did he say?

How has he spoken to you through Jesus over the last few weeks?

How have you felt sustained by God and his word during this season?

What does Jesus have to say to you today?

Reading for Reflection:

If someone wanted to tell you that they love you, what would be the best way to go about it? Would you prefer they write you a letter expressing the depths of their affection? That would undoubtedly be something you would welcome and cherish. Or would you rather they find a mutual friend, a worthy messenger, and have them relay the message to you? That would most likely be a little less desirable, but still a word you would be glad to receive nonetheless. Or would you rather hear the words of love straight from their own lips?

When you hear something second-hand it can definitely have an effect on you, but when you hear something straight from the source itself — straight from the horse's mouth, so to speak — it is a different proposition altogether. It is qualitatively different. It is so much more genuine, authentic, and personal to hear the words of affection come from the very lips of the one who is the lover.

I think that's what the writer of Hebrews is getting at here. He wants us to know that after a long four hundred years of silence, God was not content to merely send us a letter, or even a messenger, but wanted to come to us himself. Thus, in Jesus, God did something qualitatively different from what he had done in the past. He wanted us to hear the words of life and affection straight from his very own lips.

Therefore, shouldn't we take our clues from him and expect the same? Shouldn't we stop being content with merely hearing from him second-hand — through pastors and priests and teachers — and press on until we have heard his words of life and hope and love from his very lips? Let us do just that. During this season, in which we celebrate God speaking in the most personal of ways, let us quiet our hearts and our lives to the point where, when he does finally speak to us — both personally and intimately — we might actually be able to hear him.

Closing Prayer: Lord Jesus, thank you for being the radiance of God's glory and the exact representation of his being. Thank you for sustaining all things by your powerful word. And thank you for providing purification for our sins and sitting at the right hand of the Majesty of heaven; that we might join you for all eternity. Amen.

January 5
The Twelfth Day of Christmas

Opening Prayer: O Lord our God, give us a heart to seek you relentlessly, whatever it takes and wherever it may lead. Because in seeking you is our great reward — finding you and being found by you. This we pray in the name of Jesus. Amen.

Scripture Reading: Matthew 2:1-8

After Jesus was born in Bethlehem in Judea, during the time of King Herod, Magi from the east came to Jerusalem and asked, "Where is the one who has been born king of the Jews? We saw his star when it rose and have come to worship him."

When King Herod heard this he was disturbed, and all Jerusalem with him. When he had called together all the people's chief priests and teachers of the law, he asked them where the Messiah was to be born. "In Bethlehem in Judea," they replied, "for this is what the prophet has written:

"'But you, Bethlehem, in the land of Judah,
are by no means least among the rulers of Judah;
for out of you will come a ruler
who will shepherd my people Israel.'"

Then Herod called the Magi secretly and found out from them the exact time the star had appeared. He sent them to Bethlehem and said, "Go and search carefully for the child. As soon as you find him, report to me, so that I too may go and worship him."
(NIV)

Journal: What does seeking God look like in your life these days?

On a scale of 1 to 10 how would you rate your desire to seek him? Why?

How would rate your effort in seeking him?

What are you seeking with all your heart these days?

Reading for Reflection:

The contrast in this passage is pretty striking. On the one hand you have the Magi, the wise men who came *from the east* and followed the star *until it came to rest over the place where the child* (Jesus) *was.* We are not told much about them — where they were from, how many miles they had traveled, or how long it had taken them — but we can well imagine that it had been a long and grueling journey. Some scholars estimate that the travelers had ventured as many as 800 miles in search of the newborn King, which could've taken in excess of 80 days. If nothing else, these guys were serious about seeking.

King Herod, on the other hand, lived about six miles from Bethlehem. And even though he was so close to the place where *the God of the universe had just entered into his creation*, he was unwilling to go see it for himself. Certainly Herod was curious about — and maybe even a little threatened by — the stories he had heard about this *newborn King*, but he wasn't curious enough, or threatened enough — or even interested enough, for that matter — to seek the truth for himself. For some reason he wasn't willing to make the short journey to Bethlehem. I don't know, maybe he was too busy. Maybe he had too much going on. Maybe he had too many obligations, expectations, and demands weighing on him. Maybe he had more urgent, and seemingly more important, matters to attend to. After all, he had to make a living, right? He had a kingdom to run, for crying out loud. He couldn't be expected to just drop everything and run off to see this One, who *wise men from the east* had traveled hundreds of miles to see. I mean, he had far too many responsibilities to just take off at the drop of a hat and run around the countryside trying to find the One who caused a star to rise to announce his birth.

And so he sent others to go and see this extraordinary, life-changing event, while he stayed back and took care of the really important things. In fact, Herod told the Magi to go and search, and if they found anything to come back and let him know about it. He wasn't about to go through *all the trouble* of seeking God on his own. "Let someone else do the work, and then let them tell me what they find," he must've thought. What a tragedy.

Unfortunately, that attitude lives on to this day, because true seeking requires a lot of us, especially when we are talking about seeking God. In fact, it requires *all* of us. There is no half way. There is no *letting someone else do the work and then telling us what they have found.* As we talked about yesterday, it is impossible to seek God second hand. Someone else cannot do it for us. We must go. We must embark on the journey, no matter what the length, regardless of the cost. We must be like the wise men, rather than like King Herod. We must be willing to seek him, for only then will we be totally and completely captured by the object of our seeking — Jesus. Only then will we *rejoice exceedingly and be filled with great joy.* Only then will we *fall down and worship him, opening our treasures to him* and offering him all that we have and all that we are. As the prophet Jeremiah so appropriately reminds us; *"You will seek me and find me, when you seek me with all your heart. I will be found by you, declares the Lord..." (Jeremiah 29:13-14).*

January 6
The Feast of the Epiphany

Opening Prayer: O my God, teach me to seek you, for I cannot seek you unless you teach me, or find you unless you show yourself to me. Let me seek you in my desire, and desire you in my seeking. Let me find you by loving you, let me love you when I find you. ~St. Anselm of Canterbury

Scripture Reading: Matthew 2:9-12

After they had heard the king, they went on their way, and the star they had seen when it rose went ahead of them until it stopped over the place where the child was. When they saw the star, they were overjoyed. On coming to the house, they saw the child with his mother Mary, and they bowed down and worshiped him. Then they opened their treasures and presented him with gifts of gold, frankincense and myrrh. And having been warned in a dream not to go back to Herod, they returned to their country by another route. (NIV)

Journal: Put yourself in the shoes of one of the wise men. *On coming to the house* what happens in you?

What is your response to seeing Jesus?

What treasures do you want to open to him today?

Reading for Reflection:

Today is the Feast of the Epiphany. The word *epiphany* comes from the Greek word *epiphancia*, which can be translated both as *coming* and as *manifestation* (or *appearing*). While Christmas is the season that celebrates the event of Christ's *coming* in the incarnation, Epiphany celebrates the *manifestation(s)* of that coming. Thus, Epiphany is the time in the church calendar where we celebrate, and participate in, seeing the Christ. It is a time in which we must pay special attention; when we must keep our eyes open for the ways and the places Jesus is revealed, both to us and in us. It is a season of *seeing* and *recognizing.*

The scriptural focus for the Feast of the Epiphany is the coming of the wise men to *see* the newborn King (Matthew 2:1-12). It is a passage about *seeing*—*seeing* a star, *seeing* the Child, *seeing* the glory of God. The wise men *saw* the star; it is what guided them to the house. Did they see the star because they were told about it? Did they see the star because they (most likely) were astronomers and would've been trained to notice such a thing? Or did they see the star simply because they were paying attention? Surely many others noticed it as well, right? Or did they? Maybe they were so preoccupied with their own lives and problems and ambitions and worries that this strange appearance in the night sky slipped by them completely. Who knows? What we do know is that these men saw the star and it *filled them with indescribable joy.* I wonder why? It must have been because they knew that this great sight was indeed leading them to a great hope, so they followed the moving star to the place where they saw the Savior.

Thus, during this season, it might be good for us to pay attention to the things that seem oddly out of place — to people or conversations or circumstances that might be much more than they appear to be on the surface. They might actually lead us to the Savior.

Once these wise men saw the Child they were overwhelmed, so much so that *they fell on their knees and worshipped him.* Can you imagine, worshipping a newborn baby? But this was no ordinary babe in swaddling clothes, it was the God of the universe come to earth; to a lowly stable, to an unknown young couple, in the most humble circumstances you could imagine. What an entrance. It is almost as if God were trying to slip into his world unnoticed, except by those who were watching and waiting and longing for his arrival.

And you have to love the last line of the passage, that after they worshipped him *they opened their treasures and presented him with gifts.* This is the response that worship usually elicits. When we are completely captured by the beauty and wonder of a person or an experience or a moment, we tend to *open our treasures* to them. It is woven into the very fabric of our being. It is what we were created to do. Unfortunately, I often *open my treasures* to people, experiences, or moments that are not truly worthy of that offering. Only God is worthy of worship.

So, during this day and this season, what does that look like? How will I *open my treasures* to the only One who is truly worthy of them? The bottom line is: "How will I treasure Jesus today?" How will I treasure him with my time and my energies, my affections and my efforts?

I pray that for each of us this day and this season will

be filled to overflowing with his presence, his peace, and his joy, as we keep our eyes open for the many ways he will be revealed to us and in us in the days ahead.

Closing Prayer: Take, Lord, and receive all that I am and have. You've given it all to me; I give it all back to you. Do with me as you want. Just give me your love and your grace and that's enough. ~St. Ignatius

epiphany

i am here
follow the star
and you will find me
search the obscure
and hidden places
and you will come upon me
look into the eyes
of the broken and lowly
and you will discover my presence
i am here
in every conversation
you have today
in every joy and every sorrow
you will experience
in every circumstance
you will face
in every challenge
you will confront
don't ever forget
i am here

May you always know his great affection and his abiding
presence! Blessings on your journey.

~JB